NATIONAL ISSUES IN EDUCATION

GOALS 2000
━━ AND ━━
SCHOOL-TO-WORK

Edited by
John F. Jennings
Director
Center on National Education Policy

Published by
Phi Delta Kappa International
Bloomington, Indiana
and
The Institute for Educational Leadership
Washington, D.C.

Cover design by
Victoria Voelker

Library of Congress Catalog Card Number 94-61364
ISBN 0-87367-471-5

TABLE OF CONTENTS

PREFACE

Phi Delta Kappa and the Institute for Educational Leadership are pleased to co-publish the third volume in our National Issues series, *National Issues in Education: Goals 2000 and School-to-Work.* Like the first two volumes in this series, our purpose is to present diverse perspectives on how current major national education issues play out in the legislative process in the U.S. Congress.

This volume traces the Goals 2000: Educate America Act and School-to-Work Opportunities Act as they proceeded through the Congress. In articulating their diverse positions and perspectives, as in the earlier two volumes, the authors of these essays illuminate the policymaking process by explaining the development of important new national policies and by recounting the history of these two seminal pieces of legislation.

Both pieces of legislation represent new approaches to school improvement and are cornerstones of the Clinton Administration's education reform strategy. Goals 2000, in particular, embeds the national goals in legislation and institutionalizes national initiatives to improve education through the creation of high academic standards. This approach, called "systemic reform" or "standards-based reform," predicates the reform of the entire education system on these standards. As this book shows, the notion of focusing on what students learn may well be the most important concept to earn widespread national support since the equity concerns of the 1960s were translated into federal legislation. The School-to-Work legislation, in its intent to connect schooling and employment more effectively, embodies the same outcome-driven approach by focusing on occupational standards as criteria for student success.

Once again, we are indebted to John F. (Jack) Jennings, former general counsel for education, Committee on Education and Labor, U.S. House of Representatives, for conceiving this National Issues in Education series and for serving as editorial coordinator for this publication. We continue to marvel at his ability to persuade prominent individuals from both inside and outside government to contribute their diverse and valuable perspectives to these volumes.

Jack will continue this work in his new role as director of the newly established Center on National Education Policy. The center, based in Washington, D.C., is co-sponsored by Phi Delta Kappa and the Institute for Educational Leadership.

We repeat our hope that this volume, like its predecessors, will be used in classrooms throughout the country, as well as for general discussion among educators, policy makers, business and political leaders, and others interested in the shaping of education policy in our nation's capital.

Douglas Bedient
President, Phi Delta Kappa

Michael D. Usdan
President, The Institute for Educational Leadership

INTRODUCTION

By John F. Jennings

It is doubtful that the United States has ever been as deeply concerned about the condition of education as it has been for the past two decades. Presidents, governors, all sorts of elected representatives, business groups, commissions, and sundry others seem constantly to issue statements bemoaning the state of the nation's public schools.

In the mid- to late-1970s the issue was that students were not learning the basics of reading and mathematics; therefore, many states enacted laws requiring students to pass minimum competency tests in order to graduate from high school. In the early 1980s the *Nation at Risk* report crystallized a concern that, despite good efforts, academic achievement had continued to stagnate, and so students were to be required to take more advanced courses in order to graduate. As a result, many states and local school districts again raised the bar for graduation. Today more high school students are taking more academic subjects involving more rigorous coursework than ever before.

In spite of these reforms of the past 20 years, politicians and commissions continue to assert that the schools are not doing the job that they must do in order to raise the achievement of American students. And so the school reform movement continues to move in new directions.

Some reformers assert that the public schools will never change unless they face the possibility of students shifting to private schools. These individuals advocate vouchers and choice programs involving private schools in order to bring competition to American elementary and secondary education. Others contend that education must be changed school by school, and so they devote their efforts to bringing about major improvement in a single school (or a few schools) and then try to spread these good practices to other schools. Various networks of schools involving such reformers and reforms have been established in the last few years.

The school reform on which this book concentrates involves a different approach from these efforts, though it is not necessarily at variance with these other reforms. The focus of this collection of essays is on the effort to create national support for the idea of changing education through the establishment of high standards of academic content and occupational skills and then basing reform of the entire education system on these standards.

This approach to changing schools is called "standards-based reform" or "systemic reform." The fundamental idea is that once there is agreement on what students should know and be able to do — the ends — then the whole system should be oriented to achieving those ends with flexibility being given to schools in choosing the best methods — the means — to help students master these skills and academic competencies. Therefore, the keys are agreement on the academic and skill goals; alignment of teaching, assessment, textbook choice, and professional training to that content; and flexibility in all else.

The importance of standards-based reform of the entire education system is that it has been accepted at the national level as no other idea since the equity concepts that were broadly adopted in the 1960s. In that decade Presidents Kennedy and Johnson led the nation to act on the belief that the schools had to be made more accessible to the poor, the disabled, and other kinds of students who had not before been readily accepted in the schools. Various programs were enacted to facilitate the acceptance of these students: Head Start, Title I, the Bilingual Education Act, and the Education of All Handicapped Children Act are noteworthy examples. Other similar programs also were established at state and local levels.

The result of all these programs flowing from the equity movement of the 1960s is that American schools are more open to all students — the poor, the disabled, the limited-English-speaking, and others — than many other school systems of the world. So the problem of broad access to schooling has been solved in the sense that almost all kinds of students can be taught in the public schools and frequently can find special programs available to help them.

In the past decade attention has shifted to the type of education that is being provided to all these "special needs" students, as well as to all other students. Are American children receiving the best possible education? In other words, the debate has shifted from questions of access to questions of quality.

In answering those questions, the nation has groped toward accepting the idea that our 200-year-old ideal of local control of education must be changed. We now have agreement at the national level on the principle that the nation and the states must seek broad consensus on what students should know and be able to do and that this agreement on what should be learned ought to be the guiding star of public schools. It is hard to overstate this change from the past, from the reactive assertion of belief in local control to a belief that there ought to be national and state standards for what should be taught in local schools.

Since the nation's founding, local public schools have been able to define what their students ought to know. During the nation's first century, there were relatively few public schools, and so the question was not very important. But over the last century, the idea that all children ought to be able to go to school has taken root and grown, so that we have gradually moved to universal public schooling for all children. A guiding principle of universal schooling is that the locality, or in some cases the state, has the right to control what students are taught.

Now, there is a measure of *national* agreement that there should be voluntary national standards on what children ought to know and be able to do at various levels of schooling. All the major education organizations, all the major business groups, the nation's governors, the current Democratic president, and the former Republican president have all advocated this concept.

The purpose of this book is to explain why and how this agreement came about by focusing on two major legislative initiatives of the Clinton Administration: the Goals 2000 Act and the School-to-Work Opportunities Act. The Clinton initiatives are rooted in the Bush legislation and in the summit conference held by President Bush with the nation's governors in Charlottesville, Virginia, in 1989, in which then-Governor Clinton took part. At that event the governors and the President agreed on the concept of national goals for education, the first ever to be devised.

While previously there had been some acceptance of the idea that the federal government had a role in dealing with special needs children and with certain problems in education, there had not been agreement in this century that the national government had a legitimate concern about the general state of education. And, it is important to point out, the governors did not universally endorse the idea of expanding the influence of the federal government in education. Some — probably most — hoped that some new way could be found to raise the issue of education to a level of national awareness without relying on such past practices as federal grants. The tension created by trying to find this new way permeated the debate that took place during the next five years.

President Bush complemented his meeting with the governors by sending to Congress legislation that he believed would reform education. That bill contained a number of small-scale programs seeking to change a few schools and practices. The Democratic House and Senate reluctantly passed a version of Bush's bill. However, very conservative Republican senators subsequently filibustered the final bill; and the initial Bush school reform initiative died in 1990.

In 1991 Lamar Alexander was appointed secretary of education by President Bush, and he substantially revised the bill that the Senate had killed the year before. Alexander, working with Chester Finn and others who were familiar with the work of British Prime Minister Margaret Thatcher in enacting a national curriculum in England and Wales, convinced Bush to endorse the idea of national standards for education. The governors and the President had agreed on national goals for education in 1989, but they had not proposed national standards for education. Therefore Bush's second reform plan moved national involvement in education to a more advanced stage. (Readers may find it helpful to read the chapters on school reform in the first volume of this series, *National Issues in Education: The Past Is Prologue.* In that book the national debate on President Bush's America 2000 bill is explored, and the reasons are given for the failure of that legislation.)

A Republican president proposing such national standards in education was the education policymaking equivalent to the reshaping of foreign policy when President Nixon went to China. Richard Nixon had made a career out of attacking Communism and calling liberals sympathizers of that ideology; and then he — not a liberal — opened the doors to "Red" China, the same doors that he had spent 25 years locking.

Democratic Presidents Kennedy and Johnson had proposed a major expansion of federal aid to education in the 1960s and had achieved the enactment of historic legislation that created the current array of federal programs. But they were dogged along the way by criticism from conservatives who asserted that the liberals were really trying to nationalize education. Now, 25 years later, it was a self-proclaimed conservative Republican, not a liberal Democrat, who was advocating a monumental movement away from local control of education.

Despite the importance of the second Bush legislation, it ran into the same problem as the first. A Democratic Congress reluctantly passed the bill in the House and the Senate, but the conference report again was filibustered by very conservative Republican senators who were not as impressed as were Bush, Alexander, and Finn with the accomplishments of Margaret Thatcher in establishing a national curriculum.

The Goals 2000 Act, submitted to Congress by the new President, Bill Clinton, was really a culmination of several years of effort by two presidents and countless legislators, staff in the Administration and Congress, and other concerned parties. Therefore its importance can be appreciated only if this prior legislation and the struggles surrounding it are understood.

Also included in this volume is the debate surrounding the enactment of the School-to-Work Opportunities Act. While the Goals bill dealt with school reform for both elementary and secondary education (and is by far the more comprehensive of the two bills), the School-to-Work bill also is significant because it establishes a new approach to high school reform and to job training. In a way, the School-to-Work bill offers a strategy that high schools can employ to carry out the broad aims of the Goals bill.

In addition, the School-to-Work bill is included because it is the next major piece of education legislation after the Goals bill to be signed into law as part of the Clinton agenda for education. The first two items on that agenda were the National and Community Service Trust Fund Act and the shift of the student loan programs to a direct lending mode. Those two laws are discussed in the second book in this series, *National Issues in Education: Community Service and Student Loans*. Goals 2000 and the School-to-Work Opportunities Act were the third and fourth items on the Clinton agenda to be enacted.

The School-to-Work Opportunities Act also is included in this book because it is philosophically akin to the Goals bill. Both bills deal with the reform of education. Both bills also endorse standards-based reform. Both attempt to define ends to be achieved and give administrators flexibility to use whatever means they desire. Finally, both bills attempt to change whole systems, instead of funding only demonstration programs.

However, the School-to-Work bill did not follow the tortuous five-year path to enactment that the Goals legislation did. President Clinton proposed it after he assumed office in 1993, and it was enacted in 1994. But its roots are in the policy discussions that occurred at the national level during the same five-year period that the Goals 2000 and its predecessor legislation were being considered. *The Forgotten Half* report of the William T. Grant Foundation, the *High Skills or Low Wages* report of the National Commission on Education and the Economy, and the SCANS report of the Bush Administration created the fertile intellectual ground out of which the School-to-Work bill grew. While he was governor of Arkansas, the new President — and Hillary Clinton — had been deeply involved in several of these commissions.

The Goals 2000 and School-to-Work bills also are grouped together in this volume because they proceeded through the Congress about the same time, and action on the one bill affected the other. For instance, the Goals bill was thought to have a clear track to early enactment. Therefore, the authority to create national occupational skill standards was included in that legislation as it was submitted to Congress, instead of in the School-to-Work bill that was not quite ready for submission. But then the Goals bill became bogged down in controversy and imperiled the enactment of the National Skills Standards Board. Another link between the two bills was that the controversy on the Goals bill that Secretary Riley encountered as he presented it to Congress influenced the drafters of the Administration's School-to-Work bill; they changed the content of their legislation as a result. Thus the two bills not only were thematically related, they also were procedurally intertwined.

The format of this book is similar to that used in the first two books in this series. A representative of the Administration presents the President's proposal, including the reasons for its advocacy and the ways that legislative agreement had to be secured. One of the bill's major sponsors in the Congress then discusses the congressional reaction and what had to be done to guide the bill to passage. A major opponent of the legislation in Congress then presents another perspective. And, last, key experts outside the Congress give their views. At the end of these discussions I draw out some general lessons that can be learned about policy making, politics, and legislative procedures from reviewing the enactment of these two new laws.

Part I deals with Goals 2000. Secretary of Education Richard Riley discusses the origins of the Clinton proposal and its progress through the Washington policymaking process. He is followed by Congressman Dale Kildee, Chairman of the Subcommittee on Elementary, Secondary and Vocational Education, who was the bill's prime sponsor in the House. Then Congressman John Boehner, a major opponent of the bill, gives his views and explains his support for vouchers as an alternative. Gordan Ambach, the executive director of the Council of Chief State School Officers, follows because he and his organization were among the main advocates for the bill among the major national education organizations. Governor Carroll Campbell of South Carolina then presents the point of view of a state leader who supported the general concept of the bill but had concerns about the final form of the legislation. Last, Jennifer O'Day of Stanford University discusses the general idea of systemic reform and what several states are now doing with this new approach to educational improvement.

Part II deals with the School-to-Work Opportunities Act. Secretary of Labor Robert Reich discusses the concepts embodied in the Administration's proposal. His essay is followed by one written by the bill's key sponsor in the Senate, Paul Simon of Illinois, Chairman of the Subcommittee on Employment and Productivity. Then Senator Nancy Landon Kassebaum of Kansas writes about her concerns with the legislation. She is followed by Hilary Pennington, executive director of Jobs for the Future, who describes the origins of the School-to-Work concept and the possible effects of the new program.

All these writers have freely contributed their time and talents to help readers become knowledgeable about these two significant, new national policies. Literally millions of Americans may be affected in the years ahead by these laws. These essays help to explain the national policymaking process. Washington, D.C., seems very far away to many people; but what is decided there affects the lives of all citizens. Making understandable the methods used to arrive at national policies may encourage more people to participate in the decision-making processes of government.

PART I
GOALS 2000

The Goals 2000: Educate America Act. Providing a World-Class Education for Every Child

By Richard W. Riley
Secretary of Education

Richard Wilson Riley was nominated for the post of U.S. Secretary of Education on 21 December 1992, by President Clinton. He previously served as governor of South Carolina.

Secretary Riley holds degrees from Furman University and the University of South Carolina School of Law. He served in the U.S. Navy for two years, followed by employment as legal counsel to the Judiciary Committee of the Senate prior to joining his family's law firm in 1960.

From 1963 to 1967, Secretary Riley served as a South Carolina state representative and, from 1967 to 1977, as a state senator. He was elected governor in 1978 and re-elected in 1982.

When the legislative dust settles and future historians examine the Clinton Administration, they will devote a major chapter to the Goals 2000: Educate America Act that was signed into law on 31 March 1994. Like President Lincoln's Morrill Act of 1862 and President Johnson's Elementary and Secondary Education Act of 1965, President Bill Clinton's Goals 2000 Act will stand as an education beacon.

Goals 2000 takes the 1990 National Education Goals — agreed to by the nation's governors, with the leadership of Governor Clinton of Arkansas and former President George Bush — expands them, and makes them the law of the land. It provides additional financial support for states and communities working to improve their schools and to meet their own challenging goals and high standards. It offers states and

3

school districts a revolutionary management lever: a broad authority from the U.S. Department of Education to waive burdensome federal regulations. In addition, it encourages the development of voluntary, world-class academic and occupational standards that promise to help every child succeed when he or she completes school. It defines a better and more balanced role for the federal government — top-down support for bottom-up reform.

Goals 2000 accomplishes all of this without imposing a single new mandate on states and localities — and with bipartisan support through two administrations.

Throughout American history, our citizens have taken the initiative when things needed to be fixed. When Americans need to do it, we do it. Today, our citizens want better schools. Goals 2000 points the way. This statute is all about making schools safe and disciplined havens for learning, demanding standards and challenging curricula that bring out the best in all our children. As President Clinton has said many times: "There is nothing wrong with America that cannot be cured by what is right with America."

Each of these benefits will draw the attention of historians, but their real fascination will focus on a transformation that has received remarkably little attention: For the first time in the nation's history, a statutory framework defining an appropriate role for the federal government in education has been enacted. This framework defines the federal role as one of support and facilitation to improve all schools for all children, while maintaining state and local control.

Overwhelming bipartisan majorities in both the House of Representatives and Senate of the United States have approved that framework. Most of the nation's state leaders have endorsed it. It has been backed by an impressive coalition of groups representing American education, business, and families. And it has been signed into law by the President of the United States of America. That is one of the reasons Albert Shanker, president of the American Federation of Teachers, called Goals 2000, "the most important education legislation we've ever had."

This is the story from inside the U.S. Department of Education of what went into shaping that legislation, how it was enacted, and what it means for the future.

The Setting

When Madeleine Kunin, the former governor of Vermont who had agreed to serve as my deputy secretary, and I arrived in Washington in

January 1993, we stepped into a situation loaded with possibilities for the future and surrounded by pitfalls for the careless.

On the positive side, we inherited a real interest in school reform in many states. Forty-four states had responded in some way to the challenge of the 1983 report of the National Commission on Excellence in Education, *A Nation at Risk*; and some had made real, comprehensive efforts to improve their schools. Significant, but not universal, support existed in the education community for new efforts to define academic standards for all students and to measure what students know (and do not know) in core subjects at various grade levels. In addition, the academic community was contributing new theories on improving school governance and the need to fit all pieces of the reform puzzle together.

In short, we were the beneficiaries of a clear national interest in improving schools. But a challenge remained: how to transform the general interest of most Americans, and the cynicism of some, into a positive movement supporting learning. Developing the tools for such a movement would not be easy, but this became my first order of business. Here, however, we had to tread carefully, because our path was surrounded by a political minefield.

In the first place, educators had not been in on the ground floor when the National Education Goals were developed in 1989 and 1990. The goals were viewed by many as a classic example of a top-down reform imposed on localities. Some mistakes inevitably were made in developing the goals. The most serious of them, in my view, had been relying on a "National Education Summit" of the governors and the President, held in Charlottesville, Virginia, in 1989 to announce to goals. While it was a grand event, only a handful of government professionals had developed the goals, along with representatives of some key education groups. It would have been much more powerful to have had the "Summit" after a grassroots, nationwide effort to agree on the goals. Little effort was made to engage teachers or principals broadly in this very important education development.

Nor had parents, citizens, or the business community been brought into the picture in a meaningful way. Although I have never doubted for a minute that the general public supports the goals, I have always believed that if the goals are to be attained, the American people must be more than passive supporters. They must be passionate advocates.

Finally, neither members of Congress nor state legislators had a hand in crafting the goals. Yet at both the national and state levels, legislators would be responsible for shaping programs and allocating funds to achieve the goals. Without their input, how much enthusiasm for the goals could we expect from them?

All of this was on my mind as I took up my new responsibilities as Secretary of Education. Everything added up to my conviction that our new President could move national school reform forward, but that our effort to create a movement could be easily derailed.

The truth was that the reform movement at the national level had absolutely no statutory basis. Even ten years after the report, *A Nation at Risk,* there had been little federal response. The National Education Goals, three years after their announcement, had no legal standing of any kind. No federal initiatives, no funding or flexibility had been enacted to provide states, communities, or schools with the assistance they needed to reach these important goals.

Most troubling of all, as attractive as the goals were, as important as they were, as essential as they were in the final analysis, they represented nothing more than a political agreement between a former President and the nation's governors. That President no longer held the White House. Equally ominous, two-thirds of the men and women who had struck the deal with him no longer sat in a governor's mansion.

We decided to take the seeds of interest that we had inherited and transform them into a national movement — a movement in which states and local districts with a clear vision of where they wanted to go could count on the American people and the federal government as partners in the journey. Thus the Goals 2000: Educate America Act was conceived.

The Agenda and the Team

Rarely has a new Administration arrived in Washington more determined to act on education than was the Clinton Administration — and not since the 1960s has the nation seen such a flurry of education activity in the nation's capital.

The Agenda. As the new Congress convened, the Clinton team had promises to keep. In higher education, three major issues loomed: 1) The Pell grant program, the lifeline for so many college students, was in serious financial trouble, projected at $2 billion in the red. 2) The President had campaigned on a promise of making grants to college students in return for their participation in a new program of national service. We had to create that program. 3) The guaranteed student loan program was a financial and administrative nightmare, involving too many costly actors in the loan-making process. We were determined to simplify all of that with a program to make loans directly to students while cutting out the inefficiencies and costs of the middlemen.

6

Within twelve months all of that was enacted.*

An agenda at least as ambitious lay before us in elementary and secondary education. First, we were determined to promote the kind of comprehensive school improvements needed to make schools safer, more disciplined, and focused on high academic standards with greater parental involvement and more support for better teaching. In essence, promoting comprehensive, neighborhood-based reform would be the federal government's response to the National Education Goals.

Second, important programs of the Elementary and Secondary Education Act (ESEA), the major federal source of funds for disadvantaged students, had to be overhauled if students served by these programs were to reach challenging standards.

Finally, we were convinced that the time had come to enact a serious, cooperative program between the Department of Education and the Department of Labor, a program to improve the transition from school to work for the "forgotten half" — those students who did not plan to seek a four-year college degree right away.

Within the second twelve months, action on all of that will have been completed.

The Goals 2000: Educate America Act was signed into law in March 1994. It includes our comprehensive reform agenda, the Safe Schools Act, and the reauthorization and reshaping of the Office of Educational Research and Improvement (OERI). The School-to-Work Opportunities Act became law on May 4. Major improvements to ESEA have passed both the House and the Senate, and the legislation has been signed into law.

Many people have played important roles in each of these legislative adventures.

The Team. President Clinton led the way. The country has never had a president better informed about education issues. He not only knows the material cold, he understands it better than most of the people briefing him. As Arkansas governor, he had pushed through a major statewide reform measure in 1990: Act 236, which was a forerunner of Goals 2000. In the National Governors' Association, he championed comprehensive statewide reform and was a key leader in the effort to develop the National Education Goals. In announcing his platform to

---

*Editor's note: See the second volume in this series, *National Issues in Education: Community Service and Student Loans*, for a discussion of these issues.

"put people first," he made education a central part of his presidential campaign.

As one indication of his interest in Goals 2000, the President convened a meeting with me and my staff at which he, Vice President Al Gore, and William Galston and Carol Rasco of the Domestic Policy Council reviewed our plans. At that meeting, he decided to send an important signal to Capitol Hill about the significance of this legislation to his Administration: He would transmit the legislation under his own signature rather than asking me to do it on his behalf.

He followed up by asking Bill Galston to monitor the legislation and keep him informed if his help was needed. Bill Galston tells me that the President received more progress reports on Goals 2000 than on any other policy issue involving education, the environment, or crime during his first year in office.

At the department, we put together an outstanding team. Deputy Secretary Madeleine Kunin worked beside me at every step in the development of all of our key education reforms. She combined political savvy and a wealth of experience in state government with a deep commitment to do what was right for the nation's children. Madeleine also was one of the original governors who participated in the Charlottesville meeting.

Marshall (Mike) Smith, a top education aide in the Carter Administration, dean of the School of Education at Stanford University, and a member of the National Council on Education Standards and Testing, was a leading analyst calling for comprehensive ("systemic") reform. Mike signed on as my under secretary.

Challenged by the possibilities for real change at the federal level, Thomas Payzant, an outstanding leader who had been serving as school superintendent in San Diego, came on board as assistant secretary for elementary and secondary education. Nothing better symbolized Tom's commitment to reform than his track record of improving schools in three different school districts.

Two of the first people to join my personal staff were Michael Cohen and Terry Peterson, both of whom had helped me shape South Carolina's education reforms. Mike Cohen became known around the department as the "goals champion" and led the Goals 2000 staff team. Terry served as my personal advisor and counselor on all education matters at the department, as he did throughout my years as governor of South Carolina.

Kay Casstevens, the new assistant secretary for legislation in the department; her deputy, Tom Wolanin; and Rita Lewis, who took the lead in day-to-day work with Congress, headed our legislative effort. Each had served long apprenticeships on Capitol Hill: Kay as a legislative aide to Senator Tom Harkin of Iowa; Tom Wolanin as an education subcommittee staff director for Representative William Ford of Michigan, the powerful chairman of the House Committee on Education and Labor; and Rita as a key aide to Senator Tom Daschle of South Dakota.

Experienced communications professionals also joined my staff to help move the Goals 2000 legislation forward. Jennifer Davis helped to develop an outreach strategy that drew on her experience with both the presidential campaign and the National Governors' Association. Kathryn Kahler, my communications director, along with Camille Johnston and my speech writer, Kevin Sullivan, developed a communications effort that proved invaluable in rallying business leaders, educators, and parent groups to our side.

The school-to-work and OERI legislation required a great deal of additional effort and expertise. Sharon Robinson, assistant secretary for OERI, and Augusta Kappner, assistant secretary for vocational and adult education, not only made major contributions to the legislation in their own areas, but also made sure that the Goals 2000 bill, the school-to-work program, and the reshaping of the department's research effort all fit together.

My chief of staff, Billy Webster, and my deputy chief of staff, Leslie Thornton, helped to hold our efforts together while dealing with all of the other daily crises and emergency assignments that arise in a cabinet member's office.

Finally, none of our efforts would have succeeded without the diligent efforts of the career employees at the Department of Education who offered up their talents and experience to the demanding tasks of crafting, drafting, passing, and funding Goals 2000.

Our team drew on three major assets to develop Goals 2000:

- Bipartisan interest, and a serious commitment to reform on the part of many governors, chief state school officers, legislators, educators, parents, and business and labor leaders;
- New research and analysis describing the complex jigsaw puzzle of American education and the need for coherent efforts to fit the pieces together; and
- Three years of hard, but unsuccessful, work by the Congress to frame reform legislation.

Governors and Legislators Go to Work

A Nation at Risk, the report of Education Secretary Terrel Bell's National Commission on Excellence in Education, was issued in April 1983. It was one of a series of reports with a message that amounted to political and education dynamite for the American people.

"Our nation is at risk," the Bell commission reported. "Our once unchallenged preeminence in commerce, industry, science and technological innovation is being overtaken by competitors throughout the world. . . . The educational foundations of our society are presently being eroded by a rising tide of mediocrity that threatens our very future as a Nation and a people."

That harsh confirmation of what many of us had been thinking galvanized the American people and their leaders. It demanded action from education leaders across the country, and many went right to work.

From the individual and collective experiences of local and state reform efforts, several lessons were crystallized:

- Comprehensive school reform works. You can measure the results.
- Bring the public to the table, bring them early, and bring them often. In a democracy, the people rule. People — the public, school professionals, parents, and public officials — must be involved if reform is to take root and grow.
- Think big, hold people's feet to the fire, and create a legal framework for what you want to accomplish. Reform moves in fits and starts and needs the power of grassroots support and the authority of state law if it is to survive.
- Encourage as much creativity, flexibility, and innovation at the school and district levels as the system can stand.
- Provide lots of opportunities for parents to get involved.
- Honor what teachers and administrators know, respect what they do, and provide the professional opportunities they need.
- Build accountability into the system by assessing improvements in student learning and school progress.
- Deregulate in return for results.

All of these lessons were grist for the mill for Goals 2000.

The Charlottesville Goals

The state education reforms of the 1980s laid the groundwork for the National Education Goals to become the key tools for school improvement efforts in the 1990s. Marian Wright Edelman, founder and leader of the Children's Defense Fund, likes to quote the late Benjamin E. Mays, a great president of Atlanta's Morehouse College and one of Martin Luther King's mentors, on the power of goals. "The great tragedy of life doesn't lie in failing to reach your goals," Mays wrote. "The great tragedy lies in having no goals to reach."

The stage for creation of the goals was set when President Bush and the National Governors' Association convened an Education Summit at Charlottesville in September 1989. Their purpose was to develop a set of National Education Goals on which the nation's governors and the President of the United States could agree.

In the end, the participants at the Charlottesville summit agreed on six goals for American education, addressing such subjects as school readiness, high school completion, student achievement and citizenship, science and mathematics, adult literacy and lifelong learning, and safe, disciplined, and drug-free schools. Even though these goals were something clear for which Americans could reach, three years later Congress and the Bush White House still had been unable to agree on how to move us closer to attaining them.

It bears noting that the National Education Goals did not spring overnight from the Charlottesville Summit. One of their predecessors was a set of goals developed by the Southern Regional Education Board (SREB). When I left the South Carolina governor's mansion in 1987, SREB asked me to co-chair its Commission on Educational Quality. Hillary Rodham Clinton served on the SREB task force with me. During this period, Bill Clinton was a frequent participant in the dialogues convened by SREB and the Southern Growth Policies Board about how to improve education for the children in our region.

Our SREB group stepped back and asked a few simple questions: Where are we going? What are we trying to accomplish? How will we know when we have succeeded? Despite progress, the nation was going round in education circles, adopting short-term solutions and then moving on to a new fad when the latest innovation lost its appeal.

The commission issued *Goals for Education: Challenge 2000* in 1988. It presented 12 challenges in the form of goals for Southern states to attain by the year 2000:

- All children will be ready for first grade.
- Student achievement for elementary and secondary students will be at national levels or higher.
- The school dropout rate will be reduced by one-half.

- Ninety percent of adults will have a high school diploma or equivalency.
- Four of every five students entering college will be ready to begin college-level work.
- Significant gains will be achieved in the mathematics, sciences, and communications competencies of vocational education students.
- The percentage of adults who have attended college or earned two-year, four-year, and graduate degrees will be at the national averages or higher.
- The quality and effectiveness of all colleges and universities will be regularly assessed, with particular emphasis on the performance of undergraduate students.
- All institutions that prepare teachers will have effective teacher education programs that place primary emphasis on the knowledge and performance of graduates.
- All states and localities will have schools with improved performance and productivity demonstrated by results.
- Salaries for teachers and faculty will be competitive in the marketplace, will reach important benchmarks, and will be linked to performance measures and standards.
- States will maintain or increase the proportion of state tax dollars for schools and colleges while emphasizing funding aimed at raising quality and productivity. (*Goals for Education: Challenge 2000*. Atlanta: Southern Regional Education Board, 1988)

The Analysts' Contribution

In addition to the foundation established by the SREB goals and subsequently the Charlotte summit goals, we benefited from the insights of researchers and analysts from think tanks across the country. They put the U.S. education system under a microscope. What they saw was a system wherein diverse actors were motivated by different incentives that changed at different levels of government. Parents were concerned with their children's learning, happiness, and safety. Teachers worried about new demands from reformers in an environment in which they did not have the time to do their jobs. Local administrators worried about rules and regulations, trying to make them as equitable as possible for every student in the system. Business people wanted better results.

What about the states and the federal government? States were busy handing down reform mandates, often piecemeal. And the federal government was almost out of the picture.

The contributions from the research community were enormous in helping public leaders understand this situation. The Center for Policy Research in Education (CPRE) at Rutgers University worked with state and local efforts firsthand. The National Governors' Association, the Business Roundtable, the National Alliance of Business, and the Council of Chief State School Officers, among others, began speaking of the need for "systemic" reform, comprehensive efforts that would improve every part of the school system.

The RAND Corporation contributed research on teacher professionalism that was picked up by the Carnegie Commission on Education and the Economy. The National Center on Education and the Economy began thinking about the importance of states working with local districts along common lines.

Mike Smith, then dean of the School of Education at Stanford and soon to join me in the Department of Education, and his colleague, Jennifer O'Day, had captured much of this discussion by focusing on education governance. They advanced the idea that comprehensive reform depended on "aligning" incentives at each stage of government — federal, state, and local. As they put it in a major paper:

> We argue that a fundamental barrier to developing and sustaining successful schools in the USA is the fragmented, complex, multi-layered educational policy system in which they are embedded. . . . This system consists of overlapping and often conflicting formal and informal policy components on the one hand and, on the other, of a myriad of contending pressures for immediate results that serve only to further disperse and drain the already fragmented energies of dedicated and well-meaning personnel. . . . [A]ll of the energy currently generated . . . would be wonderful if it were coordinated and focused. . . . Unfortunately, it isn't.

A number of other exciting education efforts were emerging in schools and school districts throughout America. Many foundations provided critical support for these efforts and for the networks that tied them together. At the same time, education leaders were developing strategies focused on individual school change.

Analyses such as these became the core of our plan. The National Education Goals were important. They gave the country something to reach for. But if we were to reach them, we needed a strategy. Everything we read told us what it should be: top-down support for bottom-up, or grassroots, reform.

Congress Examines the Issue

As these pressures for change built across the country, the federal government was trapped in partisan gridlock between a Republican Administration and a Democratic Congress. A major reform effort by House Democrats, the Education Equity and Excellence Act of 1990, was killed by conservative Senate Republicans on procedural grounds in the last days of the 101st Congress.

In 1991 the Bush Administration's America 2000 Excellence in Education Act was introduced, calling for funding for 535 "New American Schools" and authorizing vouchers for disadvantaged students to use at private schools.

Democrats were not impressed with America 2000, either in the House of Representatives or in the Senate. They bitterly criticized the proposal to use federal funds in private schools. And they pointed to the peculiar symmetry between the 535 New American Schools and the 535 seats in the House and Senate as evidence that the proposal was little more than a political effort to distribute federal funds to every congressional district.

In politics, however, criticism is no substitute for a proposal of one's own. At the same time that the Bush Administration was pushing America 2000, two new bipartisan panels were working on developing policies of academic standards and better student testing. The National Education Goals Panel, in struggling with the issue of how to improve student achievement, began a discussion on the importance of standards. The congressionally established National Council on Education Standards and Testing, with such members as Mike Smith, Congressman Dale Kildee (D-Mich.), Senator Jeff Bingaman (D-N.M.), Congressman William Goodling (R-Pa.), and under the principal leadership of Colorado Governor Roy Romer, in 1992 produced a report titled, "Raising Standards for American Education." That report, as well as the 1990 Education Equity and Excellence Act, served as the foundation for a new initiative from House and Senate Democrats: The Neighborhood Schools Improvement Act.

The Neighborhood Schools Improvement Act promised to break new ground in federal policy, but the effort was derailed in the final days of the 102nd Congress in October 1992, when conservative Senate Republicans joined the Bush Administration in killing the bill because it was so different from the bill that they had introduced.

Enactment of Goals 2000

Thus the ground, however uneven and broken, by early 1993 had been prepared as we wrestled at the White House and the U.S. Department of Education with how to proceed.

The Political Strategy. At the elementary and secondary level, I was determined that Goals 2000 would be the Clinton Administration's first enactment, that it should precede action on school-to-work legislation and extension of the Elementary and Secondary Education Act.

Key members of Congress, particularly on the Democratic side, were frustrated after three years of wrangling about goals and the processes of school reform. They had, as one staffer put it, tried to push the neighborhood schools legislation through Congress in the waning days of the Bush Administration without a lot of enthusiasm. It was simply an alternative to the Bush proposal. With a new Democratic Administration in town, they were eager to get on with the traditional meat and potatoes of Democratic education policy — amendments to Chapter 1 of ESEA and additional funding for it.

Some House Democrats initially were disconcerted by President Clinton's recommendations as laid out in the Goals 2000: Educate America Act. They saw the proposal to define goals, standards, and reform as substitutes for commitment, programs, and money. Others, primarily moderate Democrats and Republicans, liked what they saw. Goals 2000 seemed to offer them a better, more balanced approach to educational improvement — one that promised to harness the energy of every level of government in pursuit of stronger schools and improved student learning.

It appeared to me at the time, and nothing has changed my mind since, that Goals 2000 promised to be the much more effective and balanced strategy. Our approach was to create incentives and support to encourage state governments and local communities to work on their own plans to meet challenging goals and high standards.

While pleased with the response of the moderate members of the House, we also were sympathetic to the concerns expressed by other Democrats and Republicans. We, too, were eager to revamp Chapter 1, to take action on easing the transition from school to work, to enact the Safe Schools bill, to add as much funding to these efforts as possible given the stringent budget ceilings under which we operated, and to encourage charter schools and public school choice.

However, we differed on one essential point: We wanted to do all of these things within a consistent framework that defined the federal government's role in public education and built on a shared understanding

15

that quality schools must be a national priority but that education clearly remained a state responsibility and a local function.

Hence our first critical decision. We were determined that Goals 2000 become the prism through which amendments to every other program in elementary and secondary education would be considered.

Our second strategic consideration focused on the need to give the American people ownership of Goals 2000. Here, I hearkened back to our experience in South Carolina. We had learned that neither government nor educators could reform the schools alone, or even together. The entire state had to get involved. Communities had to buy into reform. Parents had to accept standards. The business community had to support us. It was not good enough to bring parents, teachers, administrators, and business along; they themselves had to "own" reform.

Toward that end, we assembled a broad coalition of business, education, parent, arts organizations, and state and local groups to support the Goals 2000 legislation. The groups worked together and individually to activate their colleagues back home to explain and support the legislation. They, members of my staff, and I made countless speeches and school visits around the country to describe the legislation and how it fit into local and state reform efforts.

We used focus groups to test the public's understanding of major education issues, and they provided us with a consistent and essential commonsense reminder: The language of Washington often does not resonate with the folks on Main Street. Most citizens share neither the vocabulary nor the thought processes of legislators or "policy wonks." They have no interest in the causes closest to analysts' hearts — issues such as "systemic" reform or "alignment" of policy among different levels of government.

But the general public, deeply committed to education and the decent treatment of children, does respond immediately to appeals for safe and disciplined schools, high expectations and education standards, parent involvement, and better teaching. We found that in advancing Goals 2000 we needed to be trilingual, speaking the language of analysts to the policy community, the language of legislative precision on Capitol Hill, and the language of learning and its possibilities with parents and local educators.

The Legislation. The easiest way to understand Goals 2000 is to think of the statute in two parts: one oriented toward the national level, the other focused on state and local concerns. Almost all of the public discussion of Goals 2000 has concentrated on the national level. Little attention has been given to the very important provisions laying out a structure of federal-state-local cooperation to improve learning for every child in every school.

1. The National Agenda. The National Education Goals provided us with an important entry point to work with the states. Following extensive conversations with parents and leaders of the business and education communities, we decided that the third goal adopted in Charlottesville (student achievement in core academic subjects and citizenship) should have included the arts and foreign languages. With that change, strongly backed by President Clinton, we incorporated the Charlottesville goals into the legislation forwarded to Capitol Hill.

The House and Senate also improved the goals submitted by the White House. By the time the House and Senate were finished with the bill, the American people, through their Congress and their President and with the support of a broad coalition of education, parent, and business groups, had adopted eight National Education Goals (see box on next page). The national PTA was a vital supporter of the new goal on parental participation. Teacher groups, including the National Education Association and the American Federation of Teachers, threw their weight behind a goal focusing on better teaching and improved professional development.

These goals are the heart of the national thrust in Goals 2000, but other provisions include:

- Affirming the importance and role of the National Education Goals Panel, a bipartisan group made up of governors, state legislators, members of the House and Senate, the Secretary of Education, and the domestic policy adviser to the President, to monitor and highlight progress toward the goals.
- Creating a National Education Standards and Improvement Council (NESIC) to certify standards — standards being developed voluntarily, either by national professional associations or state and local groups.
- Establishing a National Skills Standards Board to certify skills standards for entry-level workers in specific occupational fields such as health care or manufacturing. Like the NESIC standards, these standards are to be completely voluntary.

2. The State and Local Agenda. The state and local provisions are completely voluntary and built entirely around achieving each state's and community's own goals and standards. Every state is encouraged to develop challenging *content* standards of its own choosing (what stu-

National Education Goals

By the year 2000:

School Readiness: All children in America will start school ready to learn.

School Completion: The high school graduation rate will increase to at least 90 percent.

Student Achievement and Citizenship: American students will leave grades four, eight, and twelve having demonstrated competency in challenging subject matter — including English, mathematics, science, foreign languages, civics and government, economics, arts, history, and geography — [and leave school] prepared for responsible citizenship, further learning, and productive employment.

Mathematics and Science: U.S. students will be first in the world in science and mathematics achievement.

Adult Literacy and Lifelong Learning: Every adult American will be literate and will possess the knowledge and skills necessary to compete in a global economy and exercise the rights and responsibilities of citizenship.

Safe, Disciplined, and Alcohol- and Drug-Free Schools: Every school in America will be free of drugs, violence, and the unauthorized presence of firearms and alcohol and will offer a disciplined environment conducive to learning.

Teacher Education and Professional Development: The nation's teaching force will have access to programs for the continued improvement of their professional skills and the opportunity to acquire the knowledge and skills needed to . . . prepare . . . students for the next century.

Parental Participation: Every school will promote partnerships that will increase parental involvement and participation in promoting the social, emotional, and academic growth of children.

dents are supposed to know) combined with *performance* standards (how well students must know the material). With the help of broad-based panels at the state and local levels, action plans will be developed to help students achieve these goals and standards, *as defined by each state and each community.* Extensive outreach will take place to gain parent, educator, and public support in the improved efforts.

States and localities then are asked to align virtually everything else in their education system around helping their students achieve their own goals and standards. Computers and other technology should support teaching to the new standards. Curriculum should be aimed at the standards. Assessment and accountability should be oriented to them. Parents should be involved in their schools and in helping their children learn. Professional development for teachers and administrators should take the standards into account. At the state and local level, Goals 2000 invites states to do what we did in South Carolina — to fit all of the pieces of the reform jigsaw puzzle together and focus on achieving a disciplined learning environment geared to high levels of performance.

A revolutionary aspect of Goals 2000 is a general waiver authority available to schools, districts, and states with ambitious action plans. In addition to this waiver authority, the legislation provides for a six-state demonstration project authorizing me to provide state superintendents in these states with complete authority to waive certain federal regulations as part of the state's effort to attain standards.

At the heart of the effort is:

- a challenge to the nation in the form of eight specific, measurable National Education Goals and voluntary national academic and occupational standards designed to serve as beacons for excellence;
- incentive funding, catalytic money to encourage comprehensive state and local efforts to define and reach for their own goals and standards with grassroots support;
- flexible accountability that emphasizes student achievement and school progress and concentrates on results, not process;
- improvement for all children — Goals 2000 is a broad, voluntary framework for all of the children of America, not simply a categorical program targeted on special groups; and
- systemwide reform that encourages states and localities to approach reform in a broad, systematic manner, rather than piecemeal.

After countless individual discussions with members of Congress, and numerous coalition meetings and committee hearings and discussions, Congress agreed with the Clinton Administration. Legislative gridlock was finally broken on the education front with strong bipartisan support.

Enactment. Three debates shaped passage of Goals 2000 in the House and Senate: 1) the role of the federal government in education; 2) opportunity-to-learn standards; and 3) the pressures of time imposed on us by budget considerations.

1. The Federal Role. Goals 2000 marked the beginning of a better, more balanced approach to school reform that said the federal government should neither control education — that is a state and local responsibility — nor ignore the pressing educational problems facing our children and schools. In the past, to deal with these competing positions, narrow categorical programs were created that focused on specific problems. The accumulation of these narrow programs, each with separate rules, was beginning to negatively affect overall education because of fragmentation and lack of focus.

I was committed to a final bill that maintained education as a state and local responsibility but also reflected the need for educational improvement to become a national priority.

Goals 2000 also established the National Education Standards and Improvement Council (NESIC) to provide world-class models of academic standards to support interested states and localities in the process of developing their own standards. Although the establishment of this panel had been recommended by a congressionally established bipartisan commission, concerns were raised about the role this new panel would play and the power it would have. To address the concerns, the composition of the panel was carefully negotiated to ensure that members of the public, parents, and business people, as well as teachers and other educators, were part of the effort. In addition, specific language was added to clarify that certification of state standards was completely voluntary and would have no impact on other educational programs. States and communities that choose to participate in Goals 2000 would have no obligation to submit their standards to NESIC.

The relationship of Goals 2000 to other federal programs also raised concerns. We at the federal level were determined to reduce barriers to communities and states in coordinating federal education programs, including school-to-work and ESEA programs. We wanted to ensure that these programs did not duplicate work for states and to ensure that children and youth were properly served. Most important, Goals 2000 had to remain voluntary, and its funding could not be tied to other federal programs. We were successful in achieving these objectives.

2. Opportunity to Learn. Along with the Charlottesville goals and the Democrats' Neighborhood Schools legislation, the Clinton Administration inherited a major political dilemma pitting civil rights and education groups, on the one hand, against conservative members of the House and Senate, business groups, and governors and legislators on the other. It was a debate that was to put President Clinton front and center on passage of Goals 2000. At the heart of the argument was a concept called "school delivery standards," or "opportunity-to-learn" standards, a controversial inheritance from the 1992 Neighborhood Schools bill.

Advocates of delivery standards complained that it was unfair to hold students to standards if the schools they attended were themselves substandard or their teachers poorly prepared. They argued that the delivery of educational services needed standards as well. Opponents, however, pointed to a different problem: the possibility that the federal government might be put in the position of making judgments about the adequacy of school resources. Despite the fact that no state or district is required to participate in Goals 2000 in any way, this concern deserved some attention.

Here President Clinton entered the picture. Republican and Democratic governors and state legislators across the country passionately opposed the opportunity-to-learn provisions in the bill reported out of the House Committee on Education and Labor. They harbored severe reservations that these "input" requirements would bring about unfunded federal mandates imposed on the states. President Clinton signaled that he could not support the House Committee version and wanted these provisions changed before the legislation crossed his desk.

After intense discussions with key Democratic and Republican leaders and their staffs, Congressmen Bill Goodling (R-Pa.) and Jack Reed (D-R.I.) helped to craft an appropriate solution to the competing proposals.

3. The Pressure of Time and the Budget. A final pressure worth noting was the issue of budgetary constraints. As Goals 2000 moved through Congress, we were facing a tight legislative deadline. The budgetary authority for the legislation would expire on 1 April 1994. It turned out that if we were able to have Goals 2000 signed into law before April 1, we could spend money to implement the program starting in July 1994. If we missed that deadline, we could not move forward for another twelve months. If that happened, even with the statute on the books, we could not begin to implement Goals 2000 until July 1995.

We went to work to get the bill done. In the House-Senate conference, Senators Jim Jeffords (R-Va.) and Paul Simon (D-Ill.) were instrumental in brokering a final opportunity-to-learn compromise. I met, as I had repeatedly, with both Democrats and Republicans to stress not only the importance of the legislation to the President, but the critical need to meet this deadline. Our supporters kept working.

Then a near-disaster happened. Senator Jesse Helms (R-N.C.) had added a school prayer amendment that was later modified in conference.

Unhappy with the result, Senator Helms began a filibuster to delay the conference report by demanding that every single word of the 231-page conference report be read on the Senate floor. It was a rare parliamentary maneuver, but a very effective threat to the budgetary authority deadline. Our challenge became keeping 60 senators on hand over the Easter/Passover weekend to vote for cloture and end the filibuster.

On that Friday I monitored the debate on the Senate floor from my office and spoke with numerous senators about the vote. My staff was on the phone with Senate offices to gather information about senators' travel plans, as many already had scattered across the country for campaign events and family commitments. As the day wore on, we began to feel like air traffic controllers tracking the whereabouts of so many senators. It was clear that it would be very close to get the votes to end the filibuster.

At ten o'clock Friday evening, after take-out Chinese in the office with my staff, we went over to the Capitol for a final meeting. Several members of my family and staff accompanied me. Everyone assured me that we had the votes to end the filibuster and pass Goals 2000. Nevertheless, we nervously sat in the Senate gallery to await the votes. Midnight was the earliest that the vote to end the filibuster could take place. As the hour passed, senators straggled in. The clerk called the roll and we tried to keep a tally. At first, several of the members we had counted on were nowhere to be seen. Our blood pressure rose. Near 1:00 a.m., the result of the vote to end the filibuster was announced. We had won by two votes. The Senate then went ahead to pass Goals 2000, 63-22. We were elated. It had been a long road to a great, great victory.

The legislation was "enrolled" (formally signed by the speaker of the House of Representatives and president pro tempore of the Senate) and rushed to San Diego, where President Clinton took time out of his vacation to put his signature on Goals 2000 — a mere 24 hours before the department's budgetary authority expired. Best of all, the President had the help of several hundred schoolchildren at the Zamorano Fine Arts Academy during the bill-signing ceremony.

Looking to the Future

Goals 2000 is now the law of the United States of America. After eleven years of public pressure for reform nationwide, eleven years of leadership efforts in some states, communities, and schools, eleven years in which analysts examined how to do it and schools developed many small but promising reform demonstrations — and after four years of congressional frustration — after all of that, the United States now has a bipartisan, coherent framework to help every child in every school. As President Clinton said when signing the bill into law, "Today, we can say America is serious about education. America cares about the future of every child."

It had been neither easy nor simple, but nothing worth attaining ever is. For more than a decade, we had to live with some disappointments; but we learned from them as well. We might have pushed something different through, but we were determined to be bipartisan and transcend business-as-usual in education policy making. And we might have worked out the legislation behind closed doors with congressional leaders; but we insisted on building a coalition of parents, educators, business leaders, and state and local policy makers — a coalition with a stake in the success of Goals 2000 *after* it became the law of the land.

When I think of the potential benefits of the legislation, however, all of the effort was worthwhile. Goals 2000 is nothing less than landmark legislation, as important in its own way as the Morrill Act and the Elementary and Secondary Education Act. The President captured the significance of the statute in remarks he made at a White House event celebrating enactment of Goals 2000 on 16 May 1994. "We must remember this," he said. "Goals 2000 is a new way of doing business in America. It represents the direction our government must take in many problems in the 21st century."

Senator Daniel Inouye of Hawaii echoed those sentiments in commenting on the award of the first Goals 2000 funds to his state on the 50th anniversary of the G.I. Bill: "This is the new G.I. Bill. It's a bill for all Americans. And I think 50 years from now we will be observing this moment, when Goals 2000 became a reality."

If the federal government does nothing else in education in the foreseeable future, Goals 2000 is a monumental enactment simply because it encourages comprehensive, community-based reform aimed at safe, well-disciplined schools and high academic and occupational achievement and provides yardsticks against which states and localities can measure their progress. This statute offers the catalytic funding, partnerships, and flexibility needed to encourage local and state improvement efforts throughout the United States.

Equally significant federal education legislation is being totally revised to fit this new approach of reform built around high standards and community participation.

The department, for example, rewrote Chapter 1 of the Elementary and Secondary Education Act so that this critical legislation, now renamed Title I, is compatible with Goals 2000. Title I, the largest program of federal aid to elementary and secondary education, will itself become part of the educational improvement agenda aimed at challenging state and local standards. Title I is no longer a narrow, remedial pull-out program. The new orientation of Title I will help eligible students meet the challenging state and local standards promoted by Goals 2000. Moreover, a major professional development program has been added to federal efforts, a new Title II, to help teachers teach to these high standards.

In similar fashion, the school-to-work legislation tracks Goals 2000. The basic issue for career-oriented students in high school is how to create incentives for high performance for students who do not plan immediately to enter college. The occupational skills standards to be developed under Goals 2000 will mean that teenagers can, under the school-to-work legislation, basically "major" in an occupation and combine classroom work with on-the-job experience in, for example, manufacturing technologies or health care. At the same time, career-oriented students will receive an education of such high quality that they can be assured of entry into a two- or four-year college if their interests change several years down the road.

Our basic idea in both Title I and school-to-work is to encourage states and localities to move toward helping all children reach for high standards. Again, Goals 2000 is the basic framework defining a more balanced and less intrusive federal role.

Goals 2000 is important on other levels as well. On the political level, I like to think our work with the House and Senate (both Republicans and Democrats) on this legislation helped to restore the civility that the framers of the Constitution intended between Congress and the Executive Branch. On our arrival at the department, we inherited decades of congressional mistrust of the Executive Branch and years of White House misgivings about Congress. While some creative tension between the two branches of government is healthy and desirable, tension of the kind that previously existed prevented the two branches from working together effectively.

Goals 2000 began to build bridges of trust. Congress and the Administration moved with impressive speed and a sure grasp of substance. Introduced in April 1993, the legislation improved during the congressional process and was signed into law 11 months later. This process proves that when Congress and the White House and their staffs work together, they can move very quickly.

Congress and the Clinton Administration knew that education should unite America, not divide it. "I ran for president not to pull this country to the right or the left," President Clinton said on May 16, "but to move it forward, to get people together . . . to face the problems, to deal with the issues."

Public support for movement was evident at the May White House event celebrating the passage of Goals 2000. More than 1,000 people from all over America arrived on very short notice, at their own expense, to participate. As President Clinton said that day, "I know the reason it has a good chance to work is because of you, and the thousands and thousands like you who have been out there working on these same issues that are finally codified into law after ten or more years."

What united the Clinton team and members of Congress was the heartfelt conviction that citizens of the United States have been correct for 200 years in believing that every child is entitled to a first-class education. That is the conviction that lies at the core of Goals 2000.

Enacting Goals 2000: Educate America Act

By Congressman Dale E. Kildee

Dale E. Kildee, a Democrat, represents the 9th Congressional District in Michigan. He is a member of the House Committee on Education and Labor and chairs the Subcommittee on Elementary, Secondary, and Vocational Education.

Mr. Kildee holds degrees from the Sacred Heart Seminary and the University of Michigan. He was a high school teacher prior to being elected in 1964 to the Michigan House of Representatives. He was re-elected to four terms in the Michigan House and then, in 1974, was elected to the Michigan Senate.

Mr. Kildee was first elected to the U.S. House of Representatives in 1976 and represented Michigan's 7th Congressional District until 1992, when he was elected to represent the 9th Congressional District.

As the first national school reform bill to be enacted into law by the Congress, the Goals 2000: Educate America Act has a unique place in the history of federal education law. For the first time ever, the Congress debated and approved legislation putting in place a national framework to support state and local efforts to improve our schools.

This national framework is important because we live in a highly mobile society where students educated in Michigan or New York may find employment in Texas or California. In a global economy it is in our national interest that all students are educated to high levels. At the same time, local control of education is the bedrock of our nation's education policy, and the Goals 2000 framework respects this.

Because Goals 2000 proposed a new role for federal education policy, its provisions were debated extensively. Much of that debate focused on how it would affect student learning, particularly for special needs students who had traditionally been the focus of federal education aid.

27

Consideration of Goals 2000 in the House of Representatives was largely a battle of perceptions — perceptions about the consequences of the bill, perceptions about the effects of various amendments, and perceptions about the top priority for education in the 103rd Congress. Its enactment was primarily the result of two factors: 1) the willingness of Richard Riley, the Secretary of Education, to work with members of the House Subcommittee on Elementary, Secondary, and Vocational Education at key points along the way, and 2) the desire of Subcommittee Democrats to give their new Administration a legislative victory in spite of diverse personal views about the legislation. As Chairman of the Subcommittee on Elementary, Secondary, and Vocational Education, I was the primary sponsor of Goals 2000 (H.R. 1804) in the House of Representatives. As the bill moved through the Congress, my role was principally to serve as a broker between the Administration and the members of my subcommittee.

Setting the Stage

Within the Congress, subcommittees are where the majority of business is conducted and where most decisions on legislation are made. The Elementary, Secondary, and Vocational Education (ESVE) Subcommittee, which has jurisdiction over most federal programs for elementary and secondary education, was where the Goals 2000 legislation was first considered.

Historically, members of the ESVE Subcommittee have been strong advocates for channeling as much federal education funding as possible to the local level while resisting efforts to divert funds for state-level activities. This is a result, in part, of the fact that congressional districts cover smaller areas within states, and House members generally keep close contact with their local school superintendents and teachers.

The primary interest of the subcommittee members coming into the 103rd Congress was the reauthorization of the Elementary and Secondary Education Act of 1965 (ESEA) and related programs that provide most of the federal education funds for K-12 education. With the election of President Bill Clinton, the Democrats on the subcommittee were hopeful. After 12 years of trying to protect federal education programs from generally unfriendly Administrations, we had a President and a Secretary of Education who were strong advocates for education. Finally there would be an opportunity to be proactive in education. The ESEA reauthorization had the potential to be one of the most significant reauthorizations since 1965, when the Act was originally enacted.

The Clinton Administration, on the other hand, arrived in Washington in January 1993 with a different orientation and different priorities. President Clinton and Secretary Riley are both former governors. Secretary Riley headed a task force of the Southern Regional Education Board that developed education goals for Southern states that would become the model for the National Education Goals. President Clinton participated in the Charlottesville meeting in 1989, at which the governors and then-President George Bush began the process that led to the National Education Goals. Their orientation clearly was toward the states, and they truly believed that the most effective thing the federal government could do to help schools was to work with states to promote standards-based, systemic education reform. President Clinton and Secretary Riley were closely aligned with the National Governors' Association and with the business community, two entities that traditionally had not worked closely with the subcommittee in the area of education. The ESEA was not a major focus of the Clinton Administration at that time.

In addition to differing priorities, the Administration did not fully understand the political baggage that systemic reform carried among Democrats on the subcommittee. During the 102nd Congress, the issue became identified with then-President Bush after then-Secretary of Education Lamar Alexander agreed to work on a systemic reform proposal being developed in the House as an alternative to the Bush Administration's America 2000 initiative.

Furthermore, while several states were experimenting with systemic education reform, there was no visible grassroots support for the concept. At the federal level, the support for school reform came from a coalition of academics, the National Governors' Association, business, and some education leaders. Subcommittee members were not getting calls from local school superintendents, teachers, or parents in their districts urging the federal government to support education reform. Public opinion data indicated that while the public in general thought education as a whole was deficient, many individuals believed the school their own children attended was fine.

Finally, and most important, many Democrats on the subcommittee feared that the needs of poor and low-achieving students would be overlooked in a standards-based education system.

Neighborhood Schools Improvement Act

Systemic reform was first considered by the subcommittee during the 102nd Congress as an alternative to the Bush Administration's America

2000 proposal. After the Charlottesville summit, President Bush proposed legislation, called America 2000, as a means to meet the National Education Goals. The proposal consisted of 13 initiatives, the most significant of which would establish a grant program to support one "break-the-mold" New American School in each congressional district (535 schools in all, including one for each senator, or roughly 0.6% of the public schools in the nation). America 2000 also proposed federal support for public and private school choice initiatives.

Rightly or wrongly, America 2000 was viewed more as a political document than as a realistic reform initiative (a view that was reinforced when the Administration proposed significantly more resources the following year for school choice than for New American Schools). However, past experience indicated that the Congress needed to respond on the issue of school reform; and since there was insufficient support for the Bush Administration proposal, an alternative was necessary.

At the same time that America 2000 was being proposed, a number of groups were proposing the use of education standards and testing as a way to improve schools. Standards and testing also were suggested as a means to measure progress toward achieving the National Education Goals. Additionally, some organizations, such as the National Council of Teachers of Mathematics, had begun developing education standards in specific subject areas.

To provide a focus for a national debate on the issue, and to ensure broad public input, the Congress established a bipartisan National Council on Education Standards and Testing (NCEST). The council's charge was to advise the American people on the feasibility and desirability of national standards and testing. I served as one of the four congressional representatives on the council. This was the first time any members of Congress were substantively included in any of the national discussions regarding education goals, standards, or assessments. The council's report, issued in January 1992, concluded that a voluntary system of standards and assessments was an appropriate focal point in ongoing education reform.

The Neighborhood Schools Improvement Act was the legislation introduced as a congressional response to America 2000. As originally introduced, it proposed a single grant program for state and locally developed systemic school reform that would encompass the entire education system. It was later modified to respond to the NCEST report by proposing to statutorily establish the National Education Goals Panel and a new National Education Standards and Assessment Council. These entities were to promote the development of three types of voluntary standards at both the national and state levels to assist states and local communities as they developed their own school reform initiatives. The types of voluntary standards were content standards describing the knowledge and skills that all children should have in specific academic subject areas at certain grade levels, student performance standards describing how well students have mastered the subject matter in the content standards, and school delivery standards describing the capacity and performance of schools in educating their students in the subject matter set out in the content standards.

The House and Senate passed different versions of the Neighborhood Schools Improvement Act and worked out a conference agreement that was approved in the House. The bill died when the Senate failed by one vote to invoke cloture and consequently did not vote on the conference agreement. However, the issues debated during consideration of this legislation did not die with the bill. They would frame much of the debate on Goals 2000.

Introduction of Goals 2000

When Secretary Riley approached William Ford, chairman of the full Education and Labor Committee, and me about moving the Goals 2000 legislation as a separate bill before the Elementary and Secondary Education Act reauthorization, we were eager to cooperate with the new Administration. We were willing to set aside any personal reservations we may have had and try to move the legislation quickly. However, the liberal Democrats on the subcommittee, while indicating they wanted to support the Administration's proposal, also wanted adequate time to consider amendments.

A meeting of the Democratic caucus of the subcommittee to discuss the bill and the possible schedule for its consideration did not go smoothly. There was strong resentment that the subcommittee was being asked to move Goals 2000 before the ESEA, and questions were raised about how the two pieces of legislation were related, including the potential impact of Goals 2000 on ESEA funding. Members were particularly concerned about the department's seeming lack of sensitivity to their views on school delivery or opportunity-to-learn standards.

It was not clear at the time whether the Secretary of Education was entirely aware of just how serious the concerns of the liberal subcommittee members were or the implications of these concerns for the future of the legislation. To his credit, however, when I called him to discuss the situation, Secretary Riley was willing to share with the subcommittee members a copy of the draft legislation that the department had sent to the Office of Management and Budget, the federal agency that coordinates policy for the White House. He further agreed to meet with the Democratic members of the subcommittee.

The Democrats met with Secretary Riley on 23 March 1993 for a very frank exchange of views. The aftermath of the meeting was something quite unique. For the first time in my experience as a member of Congress, the Administration went through an extensive consultation process with the subcommittee members regarding the provisions of an important education bill before formally submitting their bill to the Congress.

The changes sought by Democratic members of the subcommittee centered on a few specific areas. While the Administration sought to address them in the original bill sent to the Congress, these issues would rise again as the legislation worked its way through the House. These areas included: ensuring that opportunity-to-learn standards be treated the same as other standards in the bill, limiting the role of the National Education Goals Panel to reviewing and "commenting" on standards certified by the National Education Standards and Improvement Council, changing the appointment mechanism and membership of the National Education Standards and Improvement Council, and shifting more funds from the state to the local level. The bill, as introduced, contained a number of modifications intended to address the Democrats' concerns in these areas. Additionally, the Administration agreed to include a prohibition on using new tests for purposes such as grade promotion and graduation for 5 years, and to reduce the length of the authorization from 10 to 5 years. While the Democrats on the subcommittee continued to have reservations about the bill, they all were introductory co-sponsors.

School Delivery Standards/Opportunity-to-Learn Standards

A key question in the minds of most of the Democrats on the subcommittee as the Neighborhood Schools Improvement Act and Goals 2000 were debated was, "How do you deal with equity concerns in a standards-based educational process, given the great inequities in resources that exist among schools both within states and nationally?" The answer was "school delivery standards," re-named "opportunity-to-learn standards" by the Clinton Administration, who thought that the phrase "opportunity-to-learn" more accurately conveyed the intent of the standards.

Opportunity-to-learn standards are intended to provide a means for determining whether students are failing school, or if schools are fail-

32

ing their students. It was the perceived uneven treatment of opportunity-to-learn standards in the Administration's original draft that caused the most discussion at the time the bill was being prepared for introduction. This same concern would be raised at every step of the bill's consideration from subcommittee markup though conference with the Senate.

Opportunity-to-learn standards were viewed by the subcommittee Democrats as a way for states, school districts, and the public to assess a school's capacity and performance in providing students with the knowledge and skills set out in content standards. Many members felt that, without such standards, students alone would be held responsible for low achievement when, in fact, the schools they attended might not be providing an instructional program that would enable them to reach new high standards. Subcommittee members also were skeptical of the argument that low achievement by students in a standards-based education system automatically would lead to more help for schools in which large numbers of students were not meeting state standards. Rather, they saw the student performance "bar" being raised, leaving low-achieving students, particularly those in impoverished urban areas, further and further behind.

The concept actually arose first as an equity issue in the Standards Task Force of the NCEST. The Standards Task Force was chaired by Marshall Smith, then dean of education at Stanford University and later Undersecretary of Education in the Clinton Administration.

The members of that Task Force identified four types of education standards, one of which was school delivery standards. The Task Force's report stated that school delivery standards:

> should set out criteria to enable local and state educators and policy makers, parents and the public to assess the quality of a school's capacity and performance in educating their students in the challenging content matter set out in content standards. Are the teachers in the school trained to teach the content of the standards? Does the school have appropriate and high-quality instructional materials which reflect the standards? Does the actual curriculum of the school cover the material of the content standards in sufficient depth for the students to master it to a high standard of performance?[1]

The Task Force report went on to say that without clear school delivery standards and policies designed to afford all students an equal opportunity to learn, content standards and student performance standards could contribute to widening the achievement gap between advantaged and disadvantaged students. "High content and performance standards can be used to challenge all students with the same expectations," the report stated, "but high expectations will only result in common high performance if all schools provide high-quality instruction designed to meet the expectations."[2]

There was general agreement among NCEST members that any standards developed at the national level should be completely voluntary and not binding on states. During the consideration of the panel's final recommendations, I argued for the development of voluntary school delivery standards on the national level in the same manner that NCEST was recommending voluntary national content and student performance standards. However, I was out-voted. NCEST's final report recommended that voluntary content and student performance standards be developed at the national level, and school delivery standards be developed by the states "to ensure that students do not bear the sole burden of attaining the standards and to encourage assurances that the tools for success will be available at all schools."[3]

The equity debate was not over with the publication of the NCEST report. There would be another opportunity to consider equal treatment for school delivery standards because any legislation to enact the NCEST recommendations would come through my subcommittee. The Neighborhood Schools Improvement Act called for the development of voluntary national school delivery standards in the same manner as voluntary content and student performance standards. It also provided for the development of school delivery standards in state school reform plans.

Interestingly, in the same way that there appeared to be no grassroots lobbying for school reform legislation during the consideration of Neighborhood Schools Improvement Act and Goals 2000, there also would be no organized entity outside the subcommittee arguing for opportunity-to-learn standards. Some individuals and organizations within the education community supported the concept, but the organized lobbying that traditionally accompanies a major piece of education legislation was absent.

Committee Consideration of Goals 2000

Goals 2000, as introduced (H.R. 1804), provided for the development of voluntary national opportunity-to-learn standards. At the state level, opportunity-to-learn standards would be developed in the same manner as state content and student performance standards. The first order of business at the subcommittee markup on 6 May 1993 was a bipartisan substitute to make changes in many parts of the bill. Several other amendments also were adopted, including one to add a new national education goal on professional development and another to increase the amount of funds going to local school districts. However, the most controversial amendments — the amendments that the Republicans cited as their reason for voting against the bill — were those that dealt with opportunity-to-learn.

Congressman Major Owens (D-N.Y.) offered a package of amendments that proposed to add school facilities to the list of factors that opportunity-to-learn standards were to address; to clarify that states must establish opportunity-to-learn standards before their assessment systems can be certified by the National Education Standards and Improvement Council (NESIC); to add experts in school finance, the education of at-risk students, and teacher training to those who serve on NESIC; to clarify that states should develop opportunity-to-learn standards at the same time they are developing content and student performance standards; to provide that states periodically assess the extent to which their schools are meeting opportunity-to-learn standards; and to give priority to consortia that bring together organizations and individuals with diverse points of views when awarding the grant for developing voluntary national opportunity-to-learn standards. Mr. Owens said the package reflected the suggestions and ideas of five members of the subcommittee and was the minimum that was acceptable. He stated, "We would like a partnership in this bill. It is primarily the Secretary's bill, but we think that our partnership means we should have some greater understanding of what opportunity-to-learn means, and most of these amendments clarify that."[4]

Republican members argued that the amendment was opening the door to a national school building standard, and that at some point the issue of whether a particular facility meets the standards would determine whether or not "you qualify." They raised the specter that opportunity-to-learn standards would result in court battles because schools lacked money to meet such standards. Further, they argued that opportunity-to-learn standards could backfire because states would not seek certification of their assessments if they had to have opportunity-to-learn standards first; and without certification, there would be no way to know if their assessments are equitable.

Mr. Owens responded by saying:

> [W]e should not go forward with a reform plan which does not recognize that there is a need to try to provide better opportunities

for the children out there to learn. There is a contradiction, you know, in a state undertaking the reform agenda and accepting the funds for reform and then refusing to deal with opportunity-to-learn standards in some way.[5]

The amendment was adopted by voice vote.

The second opportunity-to-learn amendment was offered by Congressman Jack Reed (D-R.I.). His amendment amended the state plan provision to require the inclusion of specific, corrective actions to be taken if a school or school system does not achieve the state's opportunity-to-learn standards. Speaking in support of the amendment, Congressman George Miller (D-Calif.) said, "I think that Mr. Reed is exactly right. We can once again set up a situation where we hand out a lot of money and people go through a lot of machinations and very little results. . . . It makes no sense to say that the goal is to go to the moon and never check out whether or not you have a launch system that is capable of getting you there."[6]

The Reed amendment was debated longer than any amendment offered that day. It was portrayed as making the implementation of opportunity-to-learn standards mandatory, and Congressman Steve Gunderson (R-Wis.) characterized it as a deal-breaker that would eliminate bipartisan support. He said, "Now, what you are saying is, in essence, that in order for a state to apply for school reform in this country, you have to have the binding language to prove that any school that doesn't meet the opportunity-to-learn standards will be dealt with, and will be dealt with accordingly by that state . . . "

The subcommittee adopted the Reed amendment by a vote of 18 to 7, with the understanding that Mr. Reed would work with Bill Goodling, the ranking Republican member of both the subcommittee and the full Education and Labor Committee, and Mr. Gunderson to see if an agreement could be reached on perfecting language before the full committee markup. As time for the final vote approached, Mr. Gunderson stated that there were a number of Republicans ready to support the legislation at the beginning of the markup, "but based on a number of the amendments — or in particular an amendment that was included today, unfortunately, some of us will not be able to support reporting the bill."[7] The bill was reported by a vote of 17 to 9 with all the Republicans on the subcommittee voting no.

Opportunity-to-learn continued to be the major issue at the full committee markup as well. Mr. Reed proposed to modify his earlier amendment to eliminate the words "corrective action" and also to address an additional concern that Mr. Goodling had raised during subcommittee markup. The Republicans continued to oppose the amendment, arguing that it would discourage states from participating in Goals 2000. However, this time they had an unexpected ally. The President had sent a letter prior to the full committee markup taking positions on a number of issues, including the Reed amendment. The letter stated: "Amendments which require States as a condition of Federal support to commit to specific corrective actions for schools that fail to meet these standards goes too far." That letter also expressed opposition to any amendments that would expand opportunity-to-learn standards, change the bipartisan balance of the goals panel or alter its composition or responsibilities, or change the National Education Goals.

Mr. Gunderson again raised the specter that the Reed amendment would lead to the federalization of education. He said, "Mr. Goodling, myself and others on this side of the aisle indicated that we would accept in the spirit of bipartisanship the opportunity-to-learn standards, because, number one, they were voluntary."[8] He quoted from the President's letter and went on to say, "So this is a deal-breaker because it kills the concept of school reform and it sets the precedent for totally federalizing issues that until now have been in the total control of states and of local educational agencies."

Several other amendments were adopted at the full committee, including amendments: to require the Secretary of Education to be an ex-officio member of the National Education Goals Panel (NEGP) if not appointed by the President; to have the President appoint the chair of the NEGP; to modify the role of NEGP to comment on proposed standards and assessments, rather than to approve them; to change the way NESIC members are appointed; and to ensure that one-third of the NESIC membership are individuals with expertise in the educational needs of poor children, minority children, limited-English-proficient students, or students with disabilities. However, once again, no Republican voted to approve the bill.

The markup process was frustrating for both the Administration and the liberals on the committee. The Administration appeared to be surprised that members continued to offer amendments on matters such as opportunity-to-learn and NESIC after they had made modifications in these same provisions in their original bill. The liberals interpreted the Administration's interest in securing a bipartisan bill as a lack of concern with the views of the Democrats on the committee. They saw the Administration continually aligning itself with the governors, business, and Republicans, while it was Democratic votes that were moving the bill forward. This perception was reinforced by the President's letter prior to the full committee markup.

The frustration was probably inevitable. The Administration was excited about Goals 2000, thought they had drafted a good proposal, and did not want it changed much. However, I have never seen a major legislative proposal enacted exactly as it was introduced. As early as 22 April 1993, in a hearing with Secretary Riley, Chairman Ford predicted that many hours would be spent discussing possible alternatives to achieve the objectives of the Goals 2000 legislation. He pointed out that this always happens on any legislation that does enough to be worthwhile. My concern throughout the committee process was maintaining Democratic votes for the bill, and I was willing to accept amendments that the Administration did not support in order to do so. I knew the members were sincere about the concerns their amendments sought to address and also realized that additional changes were probable as the legislative process continued.

Floor Consideration

On July 1, Secretary Riley, Chairman Ford, Howard Paster (then the Chief of White House Congressional Liaison), and I met in Mr. Ford's office for what would turn out to be the turning point for the future of the bill. Rumors were circulating prior to the meeting that the Secretary was debating whether he should work with the members of the committee on the House floor or with Southern Democrats and Republicans whose views were closer to his own. The Secretary started the meeting by talking about the need to move closer to the President's bill. From his perspective, the amendments adopted to solidify Democratic support for the bill in committee were eroding support among governors, business, and most likely Southern Democrats. He also expressed concern that the bill as approved by the full committee did not change many of the provisions that President Clinton had identified as objectionable in his letter prior to full committee markup.

Chairman Ford and I told the Secretary that the Democrats would be with him in the end and that he should work with the committee members. We pointed out that he would run into trouble with his ESEA reauthorization proposals and other initiatives in the future if he did not work with his committee Democrats now. By the end of the meeting it was decided that the White House would work to build Republican support for the bill and that Secretary Riley would work with the committee Democrats to address the concerns raised in the President's letter.

The Secretary's eventual success in working with the committee Democrats came in part because Tom Wolanin, a long-time Education and Labor Committee staff person who had just been appointed Deputy Assistant Secretary for Legislation in the Department of Education, helped the Secretary develop a strategy to deal with the specific provisions that the Administration found objectionable. The Department identified six specific objectionable provisions and then developed a plan for working with the members who sponsored those provisions to seek changes that would enable the Democrats to move forward as a united group. Once the President's problems were resolved, the Administration would then send a letter supporting the committee bill.

Secretary Riley had direct personal contact with each member whose amendment he sought to modify and, as Mr. Ford and I predicted, the members eventually agreed to work with the Administration and accept modifications. Working with Mr. Owens, Mr. Reed, Ms. Patsy Mink (D-Hawaii), Mr. Gene Green (D-Tex.), and me, several changes were agreed to, including:

- an amendment to delete a provision in the state plan that would have required state opportunity-to-learn standards to be adopted or established prior to or simultaneous with the establishment or adoption of content and student performance standards, and a provision that would have required that opportunity-to-learn standards developed by states address the same issues which H.R. 1804 specified that the voluntary national opportunity-to-learn standards address;
- an amendment to give the NEGP authority to disapprove NESIC actions by a two-thirds majority vote within 60 days, rather than to simply comment on those actions, and to have the President appoint the members of NESIC;
- an amendment to clarify that, in cases where the Secretary is serving in an ex officio capacity, he or she shall serve as a nonvoting rather than a voting member of the NEGP; and
- an amendment to add bill language clarifying that states did not have to have their standards nationally certified, nor were states required to participate in the state grant program to be eligible for any other federal education program.

At the same time, Mr. Goodling approached the Secretary with language he had developed that he believed would address Republican concerns with the bill. This amendment stated: "Nothing in this section shall be construed to authorize an officer or employee of the Federal

Government to mandate, direct, or control a State, local educational agency, or school's curriculum, program of instruction, or allocation of State and local resources." There was no objection to this language, because similar language had been previously enacted into law as part of the statute establishing the U.S. Department of Education. The Administration got the changes they were seeking, and on September 23 the President sent a letter to Mr. Ford supporting the bill.

Floor consideration of the bill went smoothly. Ten members of the subcommittee spoke in support of the bill on the House floor, including two Republicans. As Chairman Ford and I had stressed with Secretary Riley, the Democrats were there for the Administration in the end.

The House adopted several amendments, including Mr. Goodling's amendment regarding "federal control" and an amendment proposing a new National Education Goal concerning parent involvement. Mr. Richard Armey offered a substitute for Goals 2000, which was defeated by a vote of 300 to 130. The Goals 2000: Educate America Act was approved by the full House by a vote of 307 to 118 on 13 October 1993.

Conference

Although the Senate Labor and Human Resources Committee reported their version of Goals 2000 on 26 May 1993, it was not approved by the full Senate until 8 February 1994. There was pressure to complete the conference agreement quickly because the fiscal year 1994 Labor, Health and Human Services, and Education appropriations bill provided $105 million for Goals 2000 if the legislation was signed into law prior to 1 April 1994. In order to speed things up, the House staff prepared as much of the conference document as possible prior to Senate floor consideration. While the Senate was finalizing the conference documents, the full House Committee marked up H.R. 6, the legislation that reauthorizes the Elementary and Secondary Education Act and related programs, and prepared for House floor consideration of that bill.

Because the Administration's ESEA reauthorization proposal was designed to place federal education programs in the framework provided by Goals 2000, many of the same issues, including opportunity-to-learn, were debated in January, February, and March of 1994 during House consideration of H.R. 6. A bipartisan compromise on opportunity-to-learn, which Secretary Riley had helped to facilitate, had been adopted on the House floor and was viewed by some as a possible compromise for the Goals 2000 conference agreement as well.

However, the issue of opportunity-to-learn was to be embroiled in one more controversy before the conference began. On March 1, Carroll Campbell Jr., governor of South Carolina, wrote to the President complaining about the House version of Goals 2000 and attacking the standards provisions in H.R. 6 as an infringement on local control of schools.

In his reply, the President stated that the Administration would work to ensure that no opportunity-to-learn provisions would be in the ESEA reauthorization bill when it reached his desk for signature. He also stated his support for the opportunity-to-learn provisions in the Senate version of Goals 2000, which were substantially weaker than the House provisions. When this letter became public, House Democrats were furious. However, in the end, the letter would never be raised in any discussion of opportunity-to-learn during the conference.

Going into the conference, both the House and Senate bills proposed the development of voluntary opportunity-to-learn standards at the national level. However, with regard to the state grant program, the Senate bill was substantially different from the House bill. The Senate bill called for states to develop strategies for meeting the national education goals but did not require the development of state content standards. Furthermore, the Senate bill required only that states identify strategies for providing all students with an opportunity-to-learn, rather than adopt or establish opportunity-to-learn standards. Of these two issues, once again, the main sticking point would be opportunity-to-learn standards. The House and Senate conferees met three times to resolve outstanding issues and to affirm the staff recommendations.

After trading several offers back and forth, conferees decided, at their second meeting, to ask a subgroup of members to try to develop a proposal to resolve the differences between the House and Senate provisions on this issue. The subgroup consisted of myself, Tom Sawyer (D-Ohio), Mr. Owens, and Mr. Reed from the House; and Jim Jeffords (R-Vt.), Nancy Kassebaum (R-Kans.), and Claiborne Pell (D-R.I.) from the Senate. I acted as chair. The subgroup agreed to a compromise suggested by Senator Jeffords and myself to combine the House and Senate provisions and use the phrase "opportunity-to-learn standards or strategies." The proposed compromise was then presented to all the conferees. Senator Edward Kennedy (D-Mass.), chairman of the Senate Labor and Human Resources Committee, indicated that the Senate conferees would take it under advisement; but no agreement was reached.

Later that evening, Senator Paul Simon (D-Ill.) suggested an additional modification to the proposed compromise. He suggested replacing two factors that state opportunity-to-learn standards must address (the alignment of curricula with state standards and the capability of teachers to provide high-quality instruction in the academic areas where state standards exist) with more general language giving states even greater discretion in determining which areas opportunity-to-learn standards should address.

The framework for an agreement that I thought we had reached earlier in the day appeared to be in jeopardy. Despite a great deal of discussion, the conferees did not seem to be getting any closer to an agreement. To help move things along, I called Secretary Riley; and he agreed to try to facilitate a final resolution by calling a small meeting to discuss the issue further. Attending the meeting besides myself were Mr. Ford, Mr. Reed, Mr. Owens, Ms. Mink, Mr. Kennedy, Mr. Jeffords, and Secretary Riley. Mr. Goodling was represented by his staff. After a very heated discussion, an agreement was reached on a proposal to be presented to the full conference. The major provisions of that proposal, which were included in the conference agreement, provided for the development of voluntary national opportunity-to-learn standards that address specific factors. At the state level, school reform plans simply would have to identify standards or strategies for providing all students with an opportunity to learn, the implementation of which would be voluntary. The agreement also provided that the National Education Standards and Improvement Council can certify assessments voluntarily submitted by states only if the state can demonstrate that all students have been prepared in the subject matter in which they are being assessed.

Additionally, the conference agreement retained the House provisions for state plans to address the alignment of curricula and instructional materials with state standards as well as the capability to provide high-quality instruction in the academic subject areas addressed by those standards. However, these provisions were moved from the opportunity-to-learn section of the state plan to the teaching and learning section. The conference agreement also included the provision from the House bill that requires states choosing to apply for Goals 2000 funds to develop or adopt state content standards.

Ironically, the final hurdle that had to be overcome to get passage of the conference agreement had nothing to do with opportunity-to-learn. It had to do with school prayer. The Senate version of the bill included a school prayer amendment offered by Senator Jesse Helms (R-N.C.). There was no similar provision in the House bill, and it was agreed that alternative language to prohibit funds from being used to prevent voluntary prayer in public schools would be included in the conference agreement.

The supporters of the original Helms language in both Houses of Congress were furious over the conferees' decisions. Earlier, the House had approved, by a wide margin, a non-binding motion to instruct the conferees to accept the Helms language. Language similar to the Helms amendment also had been added to H.R. 6 by the full House after an alternative to it was soundly defeated. Congressman John Duncan (R-Tenn.) had indicated he would be offering a motion to recommit the bill to the conference committee with instructions that the House accept the Senate school prayer language.

My concern was less with the substance than it was with the procedural problem that the Duncan motion created. It was Friday, 18 March 1994. The Congress was scheduled to adjourn for the Easter district work period on 25 March 1994. If the motion succeeded and the bill was recommitted to conference, it would be impossible to get it enacted prior to the April 1 appropriations deadline — and the funds reserved for the program would be lost. Given the recent House action, a number of votes would have to be changed if the Duncan motion to recommit was to be defeated. I felt strongly that the only option was to "whip" the Democrats (a process where members seek the commitment of other members to vote a certain way) and see if we could get the votes to defeat the motion to recommit. It was further decided that when the conference report was brought up, the Democrats would talk about the merits of the bill rather than the school prayer language. The combination of strategies was successful. The conference report was considered by the House on 23 March 1994. The motion to recommit failed by a vote of 156 to 232. The conference agreement was then adopted by a vote of 306 to 121.

The Senate, after facing similar troubles due to the exclusion of the Helms language, approved the conference agreement on March 24; and President Clinton signed the measure into law on 31 March 1994. The April 1 deadline for ensuring the appropriations had been met.

In the end, the Secretary got his bill, and the liberal Democrats retained some form of the concept of equity and ensured that the majority of funds would go to local schools. Equally important for the future was the strong working relationship that had been forged between the Secretary and liberal committee members.

Outlook for the Future

Goals 2000 (and the Neighborhood Schools Improvement legislation that preceded it) represent a major departure from the way the federal government has assisted education in the past. First, it supports the development of voluntary national standards for education that will be available as guides for education reform efforts. Never before in our 200-year history as a nation have we had national standards for what students should know. Second in importance is the emphasis on systemwide reform addressing all parts of the system with the goal of improving education for all children. Nearly all existing major federal education programs are targeted to special groups of children, and past reform efforts have tended to focus on one part of the education system only, such as improving testing or instituting school-based management. Finally, there is the emphasis on achieving results with the expectation that rules and regulations will be relaxed as those results are achieved.

While the legislation does not include all that I might have wished, it does provide a solid framework of federal support for states and school districts to develop and continue school reform activities. The effectiveness of that framework will be greatly enhanced with the enactment of the ESEA reauthorization legislation. The ESEA reauthorization bill, Improving America's Schools Act, embodies many of the same concepts as Goals 2000. More important, however, is the much larger amount of money involved and the fact that more than 90% of the school districts in the nation receive ESEA funds, primarily through Title I.

As a nation, we are moving in a totally new direction; and there is much to learn. Working together, states and local communities will have to develop new academic standards, instructional approaches, and assessments. This will take time. The challenge facing Secretary Riley and the Department of Education will be how best to help states and local communities encourage and maintain the long-term grassroots support necessary for systemic change to become part of our education system.

Education is a local function, a state responsibility, and a very important federal concern. Goals 2000 respects and preserves this tradition.

Footnotes

1. The National Council on Education Standards and Testing, *Raising Standards for American Education* (Washington, D.C., 1992), p. E-5.
2. Ibid., p. E-13.

3. Ibid., p. 3.
4. See transcript, Markup of H.R. 1804, Subcommittee on Elementary, Secondary and Vocational Education (6 May 1993), p. 8.
5. Ibid., p. 15.
6. Ibid., pp. 51-52.
7. Ibid., p. 97.
8. See transcript, Markup of H.R. 1804, Committee on Education and Labor (23 June 1993), p. 109.

The Unmaking
of School Reform

By Congressman John A. Boehner

John A. Boehner is a Republican representing the 8th Congressional District in Ohio. He was elected to the U.S. House of Representatives in 1990.

Mr. Boehner, who holds a degree from Xavier University, served in the Ohio House of Representatives from 1984 until 1990.

What's in a name?

Here in Washington, sometimes a name is everything.

Listening to the Clinton Administration's assessment of their successes, invariably you will hear the Goals 2000: Educate America Act listed as one of their biggest achievements.

The Educate America Act sounds great. The only problem is that this legislation has very little to do with educating America. The bill would be far more appropriately titled the "Education Status Quo Protection Act of 1993."

You see, what the name "Goals 2000" doesn't tell you is that this bill is just a promotion of the failed education status quo. It also does not reveal how its noble beginnings were betrayed by special interests and the liberal defenders of the education establishment. The sad story of how Congress undermined education reform is what this chapter is about.

State of Education

The current political environment increasingly demands action by our nation's leaders on the issue of education. There is a widespread belief that America's public schools are in a general state of decline and that action by our elected officials is long overdue.

47

But taking action for action's sake is not good enough. Despite decades of federal aid and higher spending for education, problems with public schools appear only to get worse. In order to reform the system, we should first understand how earlier attempts to fix our education problems have failed.

According to the 1993 *Report Card on American Education* compiled by Empower America and the American Legislative Exchange Council, a 62% increase in per-pupil education spending between 1972-73 and 1992-93, in constant dollars, coincided with a net reduction of average SAT scores by 35 points. A 7% decline in student enrollment during this same period was met by a dramatic increase in the number of teachers and nonteaching school employees, with salaries in the education field rising faster than the income of the average American. Additionally, in 1993, the five states with the highest SAT scores — Iowa, North Dakota, South Dakota, Utah, and Minnesota — all ranked near the top in every indicator of educational performance, yet have among the lowest per-pupil spending levels in the country.

One thing is clear, there is no direct correlation between increased spending on education and heightened student performance. In fact, if there is a correlation, it seems to be just the opposite; for a variety of reasons, states that spend less on education tend to perform better. Higher education spending has fueled a 40% increase in the nonteaching education bureaucracy over the last 20 years with almost no tangible improvements to student academic achievement. Yet politicians' and the education establishment's knee-jerk response continues to be to throw good money after bad.

In addition to declining academic performance, our schools are plagued by other, more sinister troubles: violence, drug use and sales, teenage pregnancy, and a host of other social ills that have made their way into our nation's classrooms. The need for reform is clear, and Americans are ready to heed calls for revolutionary change.

America 2000

Spurred to action by a public education system that was getting worse with each passing school year, many of America's leaders realized that dramatic education reform was necessary. In 1989 President George Bush convened a gathering of the nation's governors for an education summit in Williamsburg, Virginia. The governors, who were being led at the time by Bill Clinton of Arkansas, joined with the Bush Administration in an unprecedented effort to identify the problems with

America's schools and to propose a framework for solving them. The leaders' intentions were not to offer another Washington-imposed "reform," but to give a structure for bottom-up solutions generated by those with the most knowledge of these problems: parents, teachers, and community leaders.

The result of the summit was the establishment of six National Education Goals and a specific date, the year 2000, for their achievement. What made this proclamation unlike a typical government policy pronouncement was its substance: The goals were specific and challenging, were written by the men and women responsible for 50 states and 50 education systems, and included a commitment to accomplish the goals by a certain date. The result was an idea and a movement called America 2000.

Overnight, this bipartisan effort took hold throughout America. Communities across the country pledged to meet this challenge and began their own programs to embrace and achieve the National Education Goals. America 2000 sparked a new wave of school reform based on local involvement, with more than 40 states and 1,000 communities adopting "America 2000" programs of their own. Even my hometown school district outside of Cincinnati started a program they dubbed "Lakota 2000."

This list of measurable goals was a potent force that successfully harnessed the initiative and entrepreneurship of our community leaders to begin solving our nation's education problems at the local level — all in the name of our most prized resource, our children.

Congressional Action

In April 1991, President Bush introduced the America 2000 education strategy to Congress in the form of a blueprint to achieve the reform goals the governors had set.

The bill contained a multimillion-dollar block grant program for a variety of local school programs; funding for the establishment of new, "break the mold" schools; voluntary national testing; and merit pay for teachers. The bill also included provisions that called for parental empowerment through school choice.

While just one of a number of reforms, school choice soon became the central focus of the education reform debate in Washington. Probably the most controversial education issue since busing, school choice has been achieving great successes on the local level for years, from Harlem to Wisconsin. The idea is simple: Involve parents, the most important figures in a child's life, in the education decisions of their children. School choice aims to put parents in the thick of their child's education.

School choice gives parents, rather than the government, the power to choose their children's schools and introduces a powerful incentive into the education system: competition. Parents, if able to choose where to send their child to school, control the education destiny of their children. And schools forced to compete for students (and the tax dollars that follow them) either improve or suffer the death of any other substandard product in a free market.

Despite its simple logic, school choice has become the scourge of the education establishment. You see, school choice would forever change our school systems; performance, rather than government fiat, would determine which schools receive a community's financial and moral support, an idea antithetical to today's teachers' unions.

When the America 2000 legislation got to Congress, the Democrats who controlled the House Committee on Education and Labor decided to overhaul its language and remove its most innovative, if controversial, components. The result was the Better Education for All Students Act, or H.R. 3320.

H.R. 3320 was taken up by the committee in the fall of 1991; and though it was not as bold as the original America 2000 initiative, it did enjoy bipartisan support. Additionally, a compromise was struck over the school choice language to allow choice in states where the idea was consistent with the state constitution.

While not to everyone's liking, the bill contained elements that appealed to Republicans who were eager for at least some progress toward parent-empowerment goals. It also appealed to many Democrats because the bill still contained traditional approaches to school reform and, to many, did not "go overboard" on school choice.

The bill was approved by the House Education and Labor Committee before the close of 1991 and was widely expected to meet similar success on the House floor when it was to be voted on in the early months of 1992. That was until one of Congress' old bulls decided to stop the plan cold.

Yet Another Plan

One man, the chairman of the House Education and Labor Committee, Bill Ford (D-Mich.), was so opposed to the idea of school choice that the mere mention of the idea drew his ire. Despite the fact that the only choice provisions remaining in the bill would have resulted in funding only a handful of programs, his adamant opposition to any private-school choice led to his single-handed effort to kill the bill.

With the help of the teacher unions and the partisan politics of the coming presidential election year, Chairman Ford went to work to derail this attempt at school reform. Over the Christmas break, while Congress was out of session, Chairman Ford pulled H.R. 3320 and substituted his own education bill. His legislation, H.R. 4323, the Neighborhood Schools Improvement Act, bore almost no resemblance to the original bill that the committee had considered. While maintaining a superficial embrace of the same goals, it took a bureaucratic, top-down approach to reform that looked as though it was written by the National Education Association.

With H.R. 3320, according to Ford himself, "deader than a doornail," the committee approved the chairman's alternative on a near party-line vote and over the opposition of the Bush Administration. The Ford bill eventually died in a House-Senate conference as the 102nd Congress came to a close. Chairman Ford, in conjunction with the education establishment and their vested interest in continuing the status quo, destroyed any hope President Bush had of enacting education reform during his term in office.

A New Administration

When Bill Clinton was elected President in 1992, many who had fought the education reform battle were hopeful that this co-author of the National Education Goals would bring with him a vigor for getting the federal government in line with the ambitious education reform ideas of the nation's governors.

As the leader of the governors in Williamsburg, Clinton displayed a willingness to embrace the unconventional in order to salvage our nation's school systems. Shortly after he took office, he named Richard Riley, a fellow governor and an education reform crusader, as his Secretary of Education.

It soon became evident that they would indeed send to Congress a comprehensive national school reform bill. The new Administration's efforts, however, proved to be a huge disappointment for those of us interested in seeing the America 2000 work continued. By allowing House Democrats to co-write the legislation — which was introduced as H.R. 1804, Goals 2000: Educate America Act — the Clinton Administration indicated from the start that they were interested in only rearranging the deck chairs of a sinking education Titanic.

Naming their program "Goals 2000" was an obvious attempt to capture some of the success and public support for the initial plan, America 2000. However, once past the names, there is very little that these two legislative initiatives have in common.

Goals 2000

With the President's party controlling both houses of Congress, Goals 2000 quickly passed all of the legislative hurdles and was signed by the President in the summer of 1993. But the legislative debate over the reform ideas contained in the President's bill proved to be most interesting.

Goals 2000 was designed with one outcome in mind: greater federal control over education. It established three new federal bureaucracies: the National Education Goals Panel, the National Education Standards and Improvement Council, and the National Skills Standards Board. By giving greater control to "Big Brother," Goals 2000 clearly had nothing to do with empowering parents and communities.

The first of these bureaucracies, the National Education Goals Panel, was originally designed by President George Bush and the nation's governors during the 1989 Williamsburg summit to keep tabs on the six National Education Goals. An informal panel to help provide guidance to the states, the board was supposed simply to monitor their progress and to help the states develop policies to meet those goals.

In Goals 2000, the panel has officially been made a part of the federal government. Although given specific and limited powers, history shows how these agencies, once established, become everlasting, money-draining, authoritarian nightmares. Originally meant to be an advisory group, the panel has been upgraded to a full-fledged federal bureaucracy by the Goals 2000 legislation.

The National Education Standards and Improvement Council is another new education bureaucracy created by Goals 2000. This new federal agency is euphemistically referred to as the "National School Board," and there is good reason for this characterization. It is charged with certifying and periodically reviewing voluntary national content standards and voluntary national student performance standards that define what all students should learn. The board also is to certify and periodically review state content and performance standards submitted voluntarily by the states. Similarly, the board is to certify something called opportunity-to-learn standards for individual states. This board will oversee so-called voluntary standards. But how voluntary are they, considering that states must develop such standards in order to receive federal funding?

In sum, the National Education Standards and Improvement Council takes for the federal government what legitimately belongs to the states and local school boards: the power to shape curriculum and manage how education is delivered.

The third federal agency created by this legislation is the National Skill Standards Board. Stamped with the specific endorsement of the labor unions, this board is supposed to "serve as a catalyst in stimulating the development and adoption of a voluntary national system of skill standards and of assessment and certification of attainment of skill standards." What that means is this board will set standards for minimum skill levels for all sorts of jobs and industry. In other words, the National Skills Standards Board will determine what skills and knowledge students and trainees must acquire to work in certain jobs.

The reason this board enjoys the support of organized labor is because it gives them a chance to control, from a Washington-based bureaucracy, the national skills standards used in hiring, firing, and performance measurements employers will be encouraged to use.

Opportunity-to-Learn Standards

Among the most controversial elements of the Educate America Act are its so-called opportunity-to-learn standards. Opportunity-to-learn standards are a typical, big-government response to local problems. Washington, through the National Education Standards and Improvement Council, will determine the minimum standards for classroom conditions, teachers' pay, and school infrastructure. The premise of these standards is that students are incapable of learning unless they have well-paid teachers, modern school buildings with the latest in technological hardware, and textbooks hot off the presses. While I'm sure this effort will be very successful at increasing teacher's salaries, getting even more televisions and VCRs into the classroom, and lining the pockets of textbook publishers, it is an absolutely flawed strategy for bettering students' academic performance.

In the past 30 years, total spending on education has risen by 47% in constant dollars with no commensurate improvement in academic performance. With any positive correlation between increased education spending and better education for our children in serious doubt, opportunity-to-learn standards tell us to ignore the facts and throw more money at our education problems.

Opportunity-to-learn standards, the centerpiece of the President's education "reform" plan, can't help us improve our schools because they have little to do with the problems that currently exist. Sure, I would love to have fresh paint on every schoolroom wall, more computers in our classrooms, and the most up-to-date textbooks for our kids; but to blame our children's academic failings on a shortage of these items is not a very effective way to identify the root problems with America's public schools.

After all, before there were air-conditioned gymnasiums and VCRs in every classroom, this country had one heck of a public school system. Kids graduated on time, violence in schools was nonexistent, and we were the world's leaders in most every subject. It wasn't because the federal government spent billions on the education bureaucracy; it was because parents, teachers, and community leaders, as a team, were all committed to academic achievement.

The formula that worked then could work today. Answers to our education problems lie not in the cost of the textbooks or fresh paint for the walls, but within the people. If parents can be encouraged to assume a greater role in education, our nation will be better-equipped to handle our education problems. Our children cannot have an "opportunity to learn" unless their parents are totally immersed in their kids' educational needs.

Changing the National Education Goals

Another area where Goals 2000 falls short is on the National Education Goals. Although the concept of national education goals was maintained by the Clinton bill, in the end those goals were substantially diluted.

One change was the addition of an entirely new goal that essentially mandates opportunity-to-learn standards. The new goal states that "the Nation's teaching force will have access to programs for the continued improvement of their professional skills and the opportunity to acquire the knowledge and skills needed to instruct and prepare all American students." In English, the goal says that our teachers cannot succeed unless opportunity-to-learn standards are an essential component of our education system — again putting the responsibility on equipment and conditions rather than on individual effort.

There also are two new subjects added to the core subject areas formerly listed in one of the original goals. Now, the Clinton Administration has decided that all students should demonstrate competency in "arts and foreign language," as well as English, math, science, history, and geography. While I firmly believe all children should have an opportunity to become well-versed in the arts and in a foreign language, Congress and the President ought not have added to this carefully crafted listing compiled by the governors in 1991.

The additions to this goal raises some important questions: Where will future Congresses draw the line? When is Congress going to decide that another and another and another subject must be learned by all students? The entire idea behind emphasizing a limited number of core subjects was to steer local education officials in the direction of those important areas. Adding to those core subjects waters down the importance of the original concept of a core subject.

Goals 2000 "Reform"

Supporters of Goals 2000 claim their bill encourages reform by offering grant money designed to fund "reform" type programs. Although superficially described as a means to initiate and fund innovative local programs, the money is virtually guaranteed to be funneled only to those business-as-usual efforts currently run by today's education establishment — the same people who have run our school system into the ground over the past 30 years. Under this bill, funding is available for any program "reasonably related" to education reform. This term is purposefully vague to allow the same failed, faddish reforms to receive federal support from Washington.

School Choice

Finally, comprehensive school choice was left out of this bill. Ignoring this most basic of reforms, to the point of preventing even modest assistance to local school boards that want to experiment with the idea, is an absolute betrayal of the America 2000 principles. When school districts develop their own reform plans as required by this legislation, comprehensive school choice is not going to be on the reform radar screen. In fact, the bill actually discourages local school districts from pursuing school choice because any plan they propose, in order to receive federal support, must correspond with the state and federal plans written by the same education establishment vehemently opposed to school choice.

No one claims that school choice is a cure-all for our education woes. On the contrary, parent involvement is just the beginning. Parent involvement shouldn't stop with selection of a school or attendance at an occasional PTA conference. It goes much further than that. We must ask more than just whether we should encourage parent involvement, but also how we get parents involved at an even greater level.

There Was an Alternative

Many members of Congress, including myself, were wholly unsatisfied with Goals 2000. As an alternative, Representatives Dick Armey (R-Tex.), Cass Ballenger (R-N.C.), Peter Hoekstra (R-Mich.), and I offered the Parent and Student Empowerment Act (PSEA) as a substitute for Goals 2000.

PSEA was based on four principles: 1) recognizing parental supremacy over their child's education, 2) lessening the government education bureaucracy, 3) giving local communities control over education, and 4) ensuring that all Americans have educational freedom.

PSEA endorsed the six original National Education Goals and avoided new, mischievous government bureaucracies by keeping the National Education Goals Panel as it was originally intended: as a quasi-governmental entity, instead of the full-blown federal bureaucracy. The National Education Standards and Improvement Council and a National Skills Standards Board were left out of PSEA.

PSEA also aimed to strengthen the reform process. State and local reform panels would have been chaired by a governor and other local officials, instead of representatives of the state education bureaucracy. We felt that an accountable elected official, instead of a faceless bureaucrat, should be charged with the reform effort.

The reforms themselves also were more specifically directed at new ideas, rather than the status quo retreads proposed by today's education establishment. Instead of anything "reasonably related" to reform, we would have allowed funding under the bill to be used for merit schools, model schools (including charter schools), decentralized management, and comprehensive school choice. We wanted to ensure that the taxpayers' money was not used for any of the fad "reforms" that have been prevalent in the education community over the past 30 years.

PSEA also went further than Goals 2000 in permitting waivers from various federal regulations. Goals 2000 permitted limited waivers but subjected them to multiple exceptions and restrictive application processes. PSEA would have encouraged local school districts to innovate by permitting waivers from all federal regulations subject only to the Secretary of Education's approval. We believe it is better to give local communities a free hand with just some oversight, rather than tying both hands behind their backs and blaming them for our education problems.

PSEA also specifically prohibited the use of federal funds for school-based clinics and outcome-based education. It required schools to provide parents with prior written and informed consent before conducting any psychological testing or sex-related surveys. There were no opportunity-to-learn standards. Also, PSEA required schools receiving money from the program to honor the right of parents to remove their children from classes or programs they considered detrimental to their child's education.

In short, PSEA placed its emphasis on bottom-up reform and measurable, quantifiable results, instead of increased spending and more bureaucratic control.

PSEA was not only an answer to Goals 2000 but also an attempt to lay out an intellectual framework to dramatically reform the nation's education system. Although defeated in the House, PSEA offered the public a chance to see Goals 2000 scrutinized against a substantial alternative.

Conclusion

Since the fall of the Iron Curtain, the world community has rejected the ideas of socialism at every turn. Yet most Americans don't think twice about government-run schools teaching our children and deciding when, where, and what they will learn. We have the government deciding what goes into our children's minds at their most formative and inquisitive ages. We have grown so accustomed to our neighborhood schools and so gratified by our children's teachers, that we forget that the responsibility of the molding of our children's future has been placed largely in the hands of a government entity — the same government that can't get the mail delivered on time and can't get our driver's licenses to us without a five-hour wait at the DMV.

That is not to say that public education, as a concept, is necessarily flawed. On the contrary, it is one of the areas that the public sector historically has been most successful at administering. The public schools my two daughters attend are excellent, not because of some Washington-imposed opportunity-to-learn standard, but because teachers, parents, and the community are all actively and deeply committed to academic excellence. But I count myself among the lucky. Many areas of the American public school system are in crisis, and public education is fast becoming a national disgrace.

If you notice, there is no mention of a federal role in education in the founding documents of our country. The Constitution makes no reference to the establishment of a Department of Education. Was this an oversight? Hardly. As scholars themselves, people such as Thomas Jefferson and Alexander Hamilton realized the supreme importance of an education to the very survival of the Republic. Yet they did not deem it necessary to include a role for the federal government in education. They had a healthy enough skepticism of government to realize that the federal, centralized government ought not have a role in the molding of the minds of our children.

We can have all of the federal standards and boards that we want, but education in this country will not change. We can federalize the system and increase the power of the U.S. Department of Education, the House Committee on Education and Labor, and the Senate Committee on Labor and Human Resources, but these will not improve the minds of our young people. The change has to come from within the home and the community — nowhere else.

Washington cannot know what is best for the children of this nation. As a former state legislator, I can affirm that state governments aren't much better. It is up to parents and local leaders. In other words, it is up to us. Without the individual, our laws, and whatever we decide to name them, are just words on paper.

Goals 2000:
A New Partnership
for Student Achievement

By Gordon M. Ambach

Gordon M. Ambach is executive director of the Council of Chief State School Officers, a position he has held since 1987. Previously he was New York State Commissioner of Education and president of the University of the State of New York.

Mr. Ambach holds degrees from Yale University and Harvard University. He worked in the United States Office of Education during the late 1950s and through the decade of the 1960s, before joining the New York State Education Department in 1970.

Throughout 1994 I had many occasions to meet with local and state officials on education issues. At each of these sessions, the conversation began with problems from the local and state perspectives, not the federal perspective. The prominent topics were strategies for improving student performance; safety in the schools; setting higher expectations for students, teachers, and schools; student motivation; financing school improvements, especially related to equalizing expenditures; professional development; building parent and public support; using technologies; and testing and accountability. These major issues needed to be addressed from the local and state perspective, whether or not there was a federal Goals 2000 program.

As each conversation turned to solutions and the potential for a federal government role, it became clear to my local and state colleagues that each of the issues on their own agenda could be incorporated in their strategies to use the new federal statute, Goals 2000: Educate America Act. The statute is right on target with the local and state problems, not a disconnected, distant overlay. Goals 2000 is a means to help, because it offers a new partnership for local, state, and federal governments to address core issues and improve student achievement across the nation.

When the United States House of Representatives and Senate passed and President Clinton signed Goals 2000 in March 1994, their action capped nearly five years of effort to reshape the federal role in education with the most significant initiative in three decades. In August 1989, when President Bush and the nation's governors first stated their concept of national goals for education, they sparked the transformation. Beginning in 1990, and in each of the four succeeding years, the Congress and the Administrations of both Bush and Clinton worked extensively to advance new directions for federal education policy. The results of that extensive work are incorporated in seven objectives that guide federal resources that help to:

1. raise performance for all students in all elementary and secondary schools;
2. develop specific standards and expectations for higher performance by all students;
3. link academic and occupational skills for job preparation;
4. provide coherence among the separate federal education programs and link them more forcefully with state and local resources, particularly through the use of new waivers;
5. plan expanded use of learning technologies, which are essential for raising student achievement;
6. expand participation of business, community, parent, and government leaders in education policy decisions; and
7. benchmark American student results and teaching and learning practices to international quality standards.

Goals 2000 advances a tremendously ambitious agenda for the new partnership. No state or locality is required to participate, but all are encouraged to set new high expectations for themselves and to work together to achieve them. Goals 2000 relies on our highly decentralized decision making as a strength for creative practice. Through this statute our "natural" education laboratory of 50 states and 15,000 districts is stimulated and supported to demonstrate that strategies often described as "bottom-up" or "top-down" can be recast into new "side-by-side" partnerships that achieve both common purposes for the nation and specific objectives of localities and states.

States Advocacy of Goals 2000

The critics of Goals 2000 allege that the legislation is a federal intrusion into state and local decision making. They claim it leads to a "national curriculum" and will stifle local and state initiative with a clumsy federal presence. If that were true, then why were the officials with principal responsibility for elementary and secondary education — the members of the Council of Chief State School Officers — the leading advocates for enactment of Goals 2000? Why, in 1989, did they back the effort to establish national education goals and from that time forward work through the evolution of the proposed Educational Equity and Excellence Act of 1990 and the Neighborhood Schools Improvement Act of 1991 to realize enactment of Goals 2000?

The Council of Chief State School Officers (CCSSO) has long been an advocate of federal support for education, particularly favoring a federal role in initiating change, supporting research and development, advancing technology, and providing substantial support for those students, such as the economically disadvantaged or the recent immigrants, most in need of additional assistance to meet high standards for all. Beginning in 1987, council members approved policy statements on expectations for student achievement and graduation rates, prekindergarten programs, and school-to-work transitions, each of which forecast one of the national education goals. Throughout the decade the council advocated forcefully for the National Assessment of Educational Progress to provide indicators of student achievement for the states as well as the nation. In 1990, CCSSO supported development of voluntary national standards for education and multiple assessments of those standards that would help students, parents, and the public understand whether progress was being made.

The chiefs and state education agencies were involved deeply in preparation of the proposed Education Equity and Excellence Act of 1990 and the Neighborhood Schools Improvement Act, the forerunners to Goals 2000. Through the CCSSO, they helped to write and to enact Goals 2000 because that legislation embraces these principles: commitment to comprehensive strategies for improving achievement for all students; commitment to developing high standards for all students, both at the voluntary national level and at the state level; use of federal resources to design and implement school change strategies, with particular emphasis on professional development and learning technologies; commitment to new approaches for flexible administration of federal programs at the school and school-district levels; and the commitment to strengthen capacities of state and local education agencies to stimulate improvement in 100,000 schools — the entire system — and to make high performance the norm rather than the exception.

Council members debated Goals 2000 at great length in 1993 and 1994. They supported the legislation and have agreed overwhelmingly to have their states participate, because they know Goals 2000 helps their state and localities to resolve the issues they would have faced with or without Goals 2000. They know the statute substantially helps to advance education reform in their own states and provides a vehicle through which they can learn from one another while working together to improve education for the entire nation.

Steps to Enact Goals 2000

Although the journey for the Goals 2000 bill was begun about 15 months before its enactment, that journey followed a legislative path that began three years earlier. Understanding this record is important to establishing a broad base of support for the concepts in Goals 2000 and the bipartisan support for the legislation. The provisions of Goals 2000 have their origins in the Administrations of both President Bush and President Clinton. The law carries initiatives of both Republicans and Democrats in the Senate and House. Goals 2000 has the distinction of being the *only* education bill in memory advocated by *all* of the major business and industry organizations in the country, including the National Alliance of Business, United States Chamber of Commerce, the Business Roundtable, and six others. Our council, Al Shanker of the American Federation of Teachers, and Keith Geiger of the National Education Association led the education advocates with all the major national organizations signing on.

Goals 2000 owes its unique character to President Bill Clinton, Secretary Dick Riley, and their colleagues in the United States Education Department. These two former, leading "Education Governors" brought exceptional knowledge and understanding of strategies for state and local education reform to this bill. Their practice in state coalition building and in the painstaking work of one-on-one legislative persuasion and compromising was critical to the results. The story of how Secretary Riley worked through Goals 2000 to reconnect the relationship between the Congress and Administration for shaping education policy following twelve years of frayed, antagonistic, and distrustful relations of the previous Administrations and Congress is extraordinary. It must be told at another time. What matters for this account is the fit of the President's and Secretary's work in the context of a lengthy and deliberative bipartisan congressional windup before the Goals 2000 bill was even pitched.

In 1989 the governors and President Bush agreed at Charlottesville, Virginia, to establish national goals for education. The six goals were stated by the President in January 1990 and were formally approved by the governors in February 1990. However, President Bush never advanced any federal legislative proposals related to the goals during 1990. During the same year, the Congress initiated and developed a major education reform act, H.R. 5932, the Educational Equity and Excellence Act of 1990. The act endorsed the goals and provided substantial support to promote comprehensive change in schools and districts through state plans and competitive grants. After the passage of different versions of the bill by the House and the Senate, an agreed-on conference report came before both chambers on the last day of the 101st Congress. The bill passed the House on a voice vote but was blocked in the Senate on procedural grounds and by objections from Senator Helms and five other Republicans.

In 1991, during the 102nd Congress, President Bush finally advanced the legislative program called America 2000, which included endorsement of the national goals for education and proposed establishing the National Education Goals Panel in law. The America 2000 bill also established a process for developing standards and assessments of education; provided flexibility and deregulation in the administration of federal education programs; and supported $1 million in one-time grants to 535 new American public and private schools over a four-year period (first year appropriation, $180 million). America 2000 also proposed using Chapter 1 funds as a conduit to provide federal certificates (vouchers) to support the enrollment of economically disadvantaged students in private schools.

Democrats in both the House and the Senate, together with some Republicans, advanced an alternative approach to the new federal role in 1991. It was a revised version of the 1990 H.R. 5932, the Educational Equity and Excellence Act, and was called the Neighborhood Schools Improvement Act, H.R. 3320. This bill included the basic concepts of H.R. 5932, especially the focus on carefully planned reforms for entire schools and school districts with competitive federal grants to enable the change strategies. No private-school grants or vouchers were included. Action on H.R. 3320 was delayed until 1992 because Congress and the Administration concentrated on reauthorization of the Higher Education Act in 1991.

On 28 January 1992 the Senate, as its first order of business in 1992, passed the Neighborhood Schools Improvement Act by a bullish vote of 92 to 6. This action was taken after Senate votes with bipartisan majorities completely rejected amendments to authorize use of federal funds for students attending private schools.

The House passed its version of the Neighborhood Schools Improvement Act in August by a vote of 279 to 124. During the debate, Representative Armey (R-Tex.) introduced an amendment on behalf of the Administration that earmarked 25% of local funding for private-school choice programs, reduced the total authorization of the local support program by $100 million, and substituted competitive grants among states to be determined by the U.S. Secretary of Education in place of the bill's formula distribution of grants to states. The Armey amendment, a reduced-price version of America 2000, lost by a vote of 80 to 328 as a strong bipartisan House coalition joined the Senate in rejecting any use of federal grants for students in private elementary and secondary schools in this bill.

In September 1992, House and Senate conferees approved the conference report for the bill. However, only the Democratic conferees (the election was coming soon and the Bush-Clinton contest was heating) approved the report, which provided the following major changes in the federal education role:

1. The Neighborhood Schools Improvement Act supported school-wide restructuring with local initiatives designed to improve *entire* schools and *all* student performance, rather than supporting targeted population groups or categorical subjects ($800 million in the first year). Federal legislation had never done that before. The act provided that governors, state legislators, business leaders, mayors, community leaders, advocacy groups, and parents would have key roles in developing state and local reform plans. Federal legislation had never before included such a provision.
2. The act codified the National Education Goals and authorized development of voluntary national education content standards for students. It authorized voluntary national "school delivery" standards, predecessors of the "opportunity-to-learn" standards in Goals 2000. It provided funds for developing model assessments of mathematics and science. Each of these was a federal first.
3. The act provided for demonstration of deregulation by authorizing flexibility for some states and school districts in administering federal programs, yet another breakthrough in federal legislation.

The legislation advanced fundamental changes, some proposed by President Bush, others by members of both parties in Congress. The purpose was clear — use federal guidance and funds to promote educational change and improve quality throughout the education system. The House approved the conference report by voice vote on 30 September 1992 after turning back a motion to remand the bill to the conferees (and thereby kill it), which lost 254 to 166. Two days later, Senate Republicans, having received signals from President Bush's colleagues about his discomfort with the bill even though it would have codified his most noteworthy education accomplishment — the Charlottesville Summit National Goals — made certain the President never had to decide to sign or veto it. They blocked a final vote on the act; the cloture vote to stop the debate failed to get 60 votes (it was 59 to 40). The Senate was out of time in 1992. The bill clearly had the votes to pass if debate had been closed.

The Clinton Administration's Education Initiative

The failure to enact the Neighborhood Schools Improvement Act occurred one month before the 1992 Presidential election. The Clinton victory meant a fresh look at the emerging new federal strategy. As the lead item of the President's extensive education agenda, he approved and began advocating legislation with the essentials of Goals 2000 almost immediately on taking office. The transition team had laid out the strategy starting in November and prepared the basis for decisions on a bill that would later be called Goals 2000. The strategy was as follows:

First, the bill would be advanced ahead of and separate from the reauthorization of the Elementary and Secondary Education Act (ESEA) in the hope that it would be implemented a year before the revised ESEA and thus provide the coordinated framework for ESEA and other education initiatives to follow.

Second, the bill would focus on establishing standards for student achievement. This attention to desired and explicit student results would inform state and local plans and investments to improve education performance of all students.

Third, the bill would fund state and local change strategies.

Fourth, the bill would establish new "national" — rather than "federal" — entities, such as the National Educational Standards and Improvement Council (NESIC) and the National Education Goals Panel (NEGP), to promote and certify efforts to establish voluntary national standards that, in turn, would inform but not control state and local decisions on standards and assessments.

These strategies, on which Secretary Riley and the Administration worked tirelessly, were supported from the outset by the business community, the American Federation of Teachers and National Education Association, the Council of Chief State School Officers, and the National Governors' Association. Goals 2000 gathered support along the way from all the major education groups as they saw it move in Congress. The bill retained the initial core concepts noted above through very rigorous analysis and contentious debate that revised and reframed many of the provisions but did not drop them. Alterations to the Administration's proposal were made in four areas:

First, the required contents of state plans were made more flexible to ensure that each state could build on existing state reforms with a greater range of options.

Second, the most contentious aspect of the legislation — provision for "opportunity-to-learn" (OTL) standards — was resolved by authorizing each state to include either OTL *standards* or OTL *strategies.* Explicit limitations were built in to ensure that nothing in Goals 2000 would require a state or locality to use such standards, nor could they be used as the basis for a state financial equalization lawsuit.

Debates over this new provision or "term of art" — crafted essentially to represent the conditions for learning and teaching that students would need in order to achieve a state's content and performance standards — threatened action on the bill at several points in both the House and the Senate. Positions on OTL ranged from complete rejection of any reference at all in Goals 2000 (because it was not the "fed's" business), through the stance that OTL should be included with respect to state plans but not on a national level, to the position, "No OTL, no Goals 2000," meaning that unless Goals 2000 includes OTL, it is not worth passing. The resolution to keep OTL standards or strategies recognized that content and performance standards and assessment systems have little value unless there is the reality of the necessary OTL connected with them. The hard-won resolution on OTL demonstrated the Administration's wisdom in separating Goals 2000 and ESEA. Had these bills been advanced as a single, comprehensive package, it is likely that emphasis on standards of any kind would have been ditched as contentious baggage bogging down ESEA. The rest of the Goals 2000 strategy would probably have been abandoned with it.

The third adjustment was to the funding and use of assessments to be developed by states and localities. The concern was that creating new high-stakes tests with Goals 2000 money and using them before students had adequate opportunity to learn the content would be unfair. The debates led to adjustments under Title III, state and local grants, which now authorize use of funds to develop assessments as long as they are used for high stakes only after there is adequate opportunity to learn. Unfortunately, the same resolution was not provided for Title II funding of assessments. Under Title II, if funds are to be used to create new assessments (the emphasis is on new testing techniques for students who are limited-English-proficient or disabled), the tests may not be used for any high-stakes purpose for a five-year period. In this case, the intended protection against test misuse has eliminated the reason for spending the federal dollars. Why invest in new tests that cannot be used for five years?

Fourth, the final adjustment was fine-tuning the functions and membership of the National Education Standards and Improvement Council (NESIC) and the National Education Goals Panel with respect to their roles in promoting and certifying standards and assessments. These groups, particularly the NESIC, have extraordinarily complex and sensitive assignments related to the responsibilities and the national state levels for the content of teaching and learning. The final provisions ensure national advice and influence with state control. The implementation of this intention and the success of the groups will depend on the prominence and qualifications of President Clinton's appointees.

Resolving these four issues enabled the major business and education advocates to maintain their strong support for Goals 2000. (The National Governors Association finally could not reach internal agreement on the bill, and therefore fell silent at the end on support for enactment.) These advocates joined forces with Secretary Riley and the Administration to rally and sustain the support of the members for the congressional leaders.

The bipartisan leadership in the Senate, particularly the tremendous skill in floor management by Senators Kennedy and Mitchell on the Democratic side and Senator Jeffords on the Republican side, moved Goals 2000 through initial passage and then, in March 1994, through a cliff-hanging vote for cloture. The final bipartisan margin in favor of the conference report was 63 to 22. Under the guidance of Representative Dale Kildee on the Democrat side and Republican Representatives Bill Goodling and Steve Gunderson, the House supported the conference report with a strong bipartisan vote of 306 to 121.

President Clinton's strategy had worked. Goals 2000 was enacted as the leading initiative on the administration's education agenda. The bill even carried several bonuses. Goals 2000 finally accrued 10 titles, seven more than the original proposal, including authorization of the Workforce Skills Board, the Safe Schools Act, and the reauthorization of the Office of Educational Research and Improvement (OERI).

The New Partnership

In its first three titles, Goals 2000 establishes overall direction for a new local-state-federal partnership in education. It is "directional" legislation, providing a compass and funds to encourage and establish the changed course. Federal funding started at $105 million in fiscal year 1994, moved to $400 million in FY 1995, and is slated by the President for $1 billion per year in each of the following three years. These dollars are intended to provide the extra investment that schools and districts — like business, hospitals, armies, and other institutions — require to restructure themselves while they continue basic services with existing resources. Goals 2000 funds are not intended as permanent support, nor are they a substitute for other federal, state, and local resources. The impact of this legislation is in the new federal strategy for improving all schools and the relatively small but targeted "change-agent" investments.

Goals 2000 will have these major impacts:

1. Strategies for lifting the performance of all students in all schools. The purpose of Goals 2000 is to raise the level of performance of the entire student body. This emphasis on excellence and quality is linked with the continuing federal purpose of raising the level of performance of economically disadvantaged students to that of their more advantaged peers. Goals 2000 embodies the most important difference between the federal strategies of the 1960s and the 1990s. In the 1960s, when nearly all current federal elementary and secondary programs were begun, the national assumption was that the level of performance of students not in poverty was adequate and, therefore, the major need was to raise the performance of poor children to that of their more affluent peers. In the 1990s, the judgment is that the level of performance of even the affluent is not adequate for the challenges of the 21st century. Our national objective must be to raise the performance levels of *all* students and provide a greater boost in performance of poverty students so that they, too, meet the new high standards for the entire population.

Federal programs for elementary and secondary education in the post-World War II period have been categorical, each directing funds toward a particular population group or subject area. Each program has attempted to strengthen one part of the education system with the expectation that it also will improve the whole. That has not been the case. Goals 2000 addresses all schools and all students. The approach supports well-aligned strategies that link goals and standards, curriculum, materials, technology, professional development, assessments, accountability, and resources. Goals 2000 uses federal resources with the objective of improving everyone's performance.

2. *Use of standards to generate more effective student and teacher effort and achievement.* "Standards" is the word most closely related to Goals 2000. It is a term with fresh currency in education. Most discussions in the 1980s used "goals" and "objectives" in thinking about expectations for students, teachers, and schools. As attention in the 1990s has focused more on student results and with greater precision on expectations for achievement, the term "standards" has become more prevalent.

Three types of standards are included in Goals 2000: content standards, student performance standards, and opportunity-to-learn standards. Content standards refer to what students are expected to know and be able to do. Performance standards indicate the level of achievement that students are expected to attain on the content standards at various stages in their education. Opportunity-to-learn standards indicate the conditions of teaching and learning necessary for students to achieve the content and performance standards.

Goals 2000 starts with content and performance standards. The development of these standards is extraordinarily important for education. Content standards focus the education system on results rather than inputs. They establish priorities among the purposes of education and help students, teachers, parents, school authorities, business and higher education leaders, and the public to establish explicit, shared expectations for learning. The process of setting standards with all these participants is essential to enable students to meet the standards. Content standards inform the curriculum, materials, professional practices and development, and the use of technologies, assessments, and accountability systems to enable more effective results. They help to link local education agencies and state agencies.

Content standards are essential for educational equity. Because they are set for all students and establish the basis for performance standards, opportunity-to-learn standards, and the assessments of results, content standards also provide indicators of equity and so form a base on which to make decisions about the allocation of resources to achieve equity.

State and local participation in Goals 2000 requires development of content and performance standards. The law is stimulating review and action at the local district, state, and national levels about the purposes of education and expectations for students. This nationwide "conversation" is generating an important forum for connecting professional educator experience and judgment with the public's aspirations for education, as represented through political decision making. The resolutions of these exchanges will establish the level of clarity, consensus, and support of localities, states, and the nation about preparing students for the 21st century.

3. Linking academic and occupational skills for job preparation. The paths to prepare American youth for employment are uncertain. Unlike many of our international trading partners, our patterns for preparing youth for employment, particularly those taking jobs before postsecondary study, are haphazard or tied to an earlier era when manual labor was predominant. To prepare all students for a highly skilled, highwage, highly competitive international work environment demands extensive educational retooling. Several connections must be strengthened — the partnership between businesses and schools, articulation between secondary and postsecondary institutions, and the integration of academic and occupational learning.

Improved job preparation is advanced by Goals 2000 in two important ways. First, the act requires that state plans for Goals 2000 must be linked with plans under the companion federal School-to-Work Opportunities Act. (Linkage is built into that act). Second, Goals 2000 creates both the Workforce Skills Board and the National Education Standards and Improvement Council with the provision that the Skills Board includes the chair and one other member of NESIC. The work of both is to be coordinated so that standards and certifications for academic and occupational objectives under the jurisdiction of each are consistent and reinforcing.

These companion acts send strong nationwide messages that major changes must be made in the overall design and conduct of job preparation. Together, they provide the means for reshaping the use of federal funds under a variety of education and job-preparation programs and for linking business, labor, education, and government at local, state, and federal levels to prepare a workforce well-equipped with academic and occupational, theoretical, and practical skills.

4. Greater effect on student results through flexible administration. Added together, the various federal elementary and secondary education programs make up about 7% of the total of local, state, and federal expenditures for education in the United States. The federal portion is fragmented into dozens of categorical aids. The separate programs have worthy purposes, but typically they do not reinforce one another or provide an aggregate impact greater than the sum of the parts. Goals 2000 promotes coordination of federal programs for greater results in two ways.

First, it provides that a state's Goals 2000 improvement plan also may serve as the plan for most of the other federal education programs, if the state so chooses. By providing a framework for the reauthorized Elementary and Secondary Education Act, the Goals 2000 state plan, including its state standards and assessments, can serve for Titles I and II of the new Improving American Schools Act (IASA). Administrative resources for the programs under the IASA may be joined with those of Goals 2000 at both the state and the local levels.

Second, Goals 2000 provides unprecedented waiver authority that invites states to create new solutions to long-standing problems. To understand the importance of this new administrative flexibility, it is important to note that unlike the authority accorded the Secretaries of Health and Human Services, Agriculture, or Transportation, the Secretary of Education has had no authority to waive federal regulatory or statutory provisions with respect to implementation of programs under the Secretary's jurisdiction at the state or local levels. Goals 2000 opens a major window for new federal, state, and local partnerships in the administration of education programs. It provides waivers to combine several categorical services and administrative resources. Furthermore, to test the potential of a major reassignment of authority from the federal to the state level, six states may gain the opportunity to take on the responsibility to determine waivers that would otherwise have to be referred to the Secretary.

The full potential of these provisions will be realized through the creative work of state and local education agencies. This restructuring is a significant recognition of decentralized decision making, trusting that states and localities will accept responsibility for working faithfully and diligently toward explicit goals, objectives, and standards that the states and localities have set for themselves.

5. Commitment to Learning Technologies. Elementary and secondary schools in the United States typically are far behind in the use of technologies commonly found in business, industry, and, indeed, in many homes. The use of such technologies is essential to ensure that all students learn to function effectively in the information age and gain the capacity for high productivity in employment. The technological environment *in* the schools must prepare students for the technological environments *outside* the schools.

Although federal education programs have stimulated some development of distance learning and demonstrations of various technologies, no sustained initiatives have been created to assist states and localities with design, planning, and implementation of large-scale, statewide technological changes. There has been a tremendous void in such leadership at the federal level. Of the various services, tools, and capacities available to improve learning in America, the capacity actually most subject to federal policy making, regulation, or action is the use of telecommunications and learning technologies.

Goals 2000 earmarks grants to support the development of statewide learning-technology plans for each of the states choosing to apply. State education agencies also are encouraged to work with businesses and relevant government agencies on systemwide plans and in multi-state consortia. They are encouraged to explore the full range of technologies and telecommunications capacities that can bring the National Information Infrastructure and broadband capacity to all learners in all schools. The Goals 2000-supported plans are intended to set directions for the use of grants for technology now authorized in the Improving America's Schools Act.

The focus on learning technologies in Goals 2000 has had the companion effect of increasing the attention by the United States Education Department, and particularly Secretary Riley, to proactive advocacy of the use of technologies and telecommunications for learning. The Secretary's presentation before Congress in 1994 for the federal government to commit enhanced telecommunications capacity for education as an essential and integral part of public education was stunning. The Secretary's efforts have been reinforced by CCSSO and other groups urging that the new national telecommunications act include authority for the Federal Communications Commission to award a favored place for education in reservation of broadband telecommunications resources. This advocacy of using a part of the "national telecommunications treasure" — broadband capacity — and of the dedication of revenues from sale of broadband rights for education is directly linked with the Goals 2000 emphasis on achieving national goals through learning technologies.

6. Opening participation in education decision making. Goals 2000 establishes important new roles in state and the local education planning for government officials, business leaders, advocacy groups, community organizations, labor groups, parents, teachers, and students.

They have key responsibilities to advise boards of education. The commitment by business and governmental organizations to enacting Goals 2000 was related directly to their intention to participate actively at state and local levels in helping to shape education standards and to assist in providing resources for the necessary changes to increase student achievement. Goals 2000, more than any previous federal legislation, opens forums for more extensive participation by these key stakeholders.

7. *International benchmarking.* Finally, Goals 2000 sets the expectation that standards, results, and practices in our schools will be judged against the quality of education provided by our major international partners. For the first time, national policy uses an international yardstick in much the same way that we compare the American economy, or American sports or entertainment, against the quality of their counterparts in other nations. Goals 2000 does not dwell on creating a scorecard of results among the nations; far more important, it requires international comparisons of standards, practices, assessments, and results through which we may learn more about our own efforts and improve education for our students.

Conclusion

These seven effects of Goals 2000 sum up the reasons that it is such a significant federal act and represents the most significant change in federal education policy in three decades. They also indicate the reasons that the states and members of the CCSSO have so strongly supported the legislation.

Expectations for Goals 2000 results are enormous. The time between the first attempt at national goals for education in 1989 and the enactment of Goals 2000 was nearly five years. Nearly half of the years remaining before the year 2000, by which time the goals were to be achieved, had elapsed. During that five-year period was little progress on developing and establishing the federal responsibility for achieving national education goals. Although certain start-ups occurred, such as the National Science Foundation's State Systemic Initiatives (SSI), for the most part federal agencies pursued activities established in the 1980s.

During this period, many members of Congress, mainly Democrats but also some key Republicans, were skeptical — even outright antagonistic — toward the National Education Goals. They were displeased that President Bush and the governors had declared the goals without any effort to include the Congress. This feeling was especially strong among congressional leaders who had carried the federal education agenda through the 1980s, overcoming the Reagan-Bush opposition.

The enactment of Goals 2000 finally provided official endorsement of the National Education Goals. The Congress included the six goals first stated in 1989 and added two of its own, one advocating participation of parents and a second calling for adequate preparation of professionals to help students achieve the new standards. Goals 2000 cleared the air with respect to the status of the goals and united the Congress and Administration in a mission to use federal leadership. It set the framework for all future federal actions to improve elementary and secondary education.

In enacting Goals 2000, the Congress and Administration created a new resolution of the American dilemma: balancing the need to marshal the nation's resources to solve nationwide education problems and avoiding federal control of education. Our common problems must be dealt with by the entire nation. We need the means to address them together, and we also need ways for the states and localities to pool their capacities.

Goals 2000 provides an ingenious response to the sensitive task of developing education standards. Authority for academic and workforce standards clearly rests with the states and localities. The task of the new NESIC and the Workforce Skills Board is to encourage and to certify examples of high-quality standards. Voluntary standards are prepared through the work of the best experts available to the nation. Encouragement, support, and certification of quality is nationwide, but use of the standards is at the choice of the states and localities. The boards are national, not federal; they have the opportunity to raise up the nation's expectations for education and encourage best practice without federal control of the content.

The impact of Goals 2000 will depend on the creativity, the imagination, and the will to take risks by the localities, the states, and the federal government. Among our 100,000 schools, examples of the best education practices and results in the world can be found. "Cutting edge" and "break-the-mold" practices of every variety exist. Our nation's challenge is to transform the successes of some schools into the norm for all schools.

A quarter-century ago, Americans first walked on the moon and safely returned home. They did so because, under President Kennedy's leadership, the nation accepted the challenge in 1961 to reach the goal of a successful moon landing by the end of that decade. In the early

74

1960s we did not know how to do it, but that lack of knowledge did not impair the pursuit. Rather, it rallied the nation to tackle a new frontier. Let us hope that same spirit can and will be applied to the journey of Goals 2000.

The Governors and the National Education Goals

by Governor Carroll A. Campbell, Jr.

Carroll Ashmore Campbell, Jr. is the governor of South Carolina, having been elected in 1986. He is only the second Republican to be elected as the state's governor in more than a century.

Mr. Campbell previously served two terms in the South Carolina House of Representatives, beginning in 1970; served as executive assistant to Governor James B. Edwards, 1975 to 1976; and in 1976 was elected to the South Carolina Senate.

Mr. Campbell was elected to the U.S. Congress in 1978 from South Carolina's 4th Congressional District, which he represented for eight years.

When the nation's governors embarked on the national education goals process in 1989, it was because collectively we believed certain things about education reform. We believed that we needed to focus first and foremost on results — on the level of achievement that comes out of the system, and not the level of resources going into it. And we all agreed that we were willing to give schools a high degree of flexibility and freedom if they could show us the results we wanted to see.

We believed that the process should be national and voluntary, as opposed to federal and mandated. In other words, we governors wanted the same deal for our states that we were willing to give our schools, and in exchange we were willing to be accountable if things went wrong. But we were convinced that the decisions about how to implement reform should be made not in Washington, but in our states and communities, where the real work of educating children gets done.

We believed that if we gave parents accurate information by which to judge their children's performance — against the kind of standards used by the rest of the world — that they would be our most powerful partners in helping our schools to change. All parents want high-quality education for their kids. But until the national education goals, we had never given them the objective measures they need to be able to evaluate fairly the quality of the schools their children attend.

We believed that we do children themselves a disservice if we fail to challenge them to be the best. Nobody wins medals for mediocrity. But we hand out diplomas for it all the time — and then send kids into a work world where the standards are now so demanding that many of our students cannot even make it through the workplace door.

And finally, we believed that the schools cannot be the only focal point of our attention in education reform. Learning begins at birth and continues throughout life — the system must be lifelong.

These are the principles from which we started. Most of them have survived more or less intact in the five years since we embarked on this adventure, though the battles over some have been hard-fought. There are still those who believe that states (and the schools and communities they represent) will never embrace reforms along these lines except through federal coercion, such as the threatened loss of their federal funds. But most of the nation's governors — Democrat and Republican — reject that view. The governors stand overwhelmingly for the preeminent role of states, communities, individual schools, and parents; and many of them are proving in their states just how powerful voluntary reform can be. What follows is the story of our role, from the setting of the National Education Goals to the passage of Goals 2000 and the systemic education reform efforts now going on in many states. This is a story that is told from the point of view of states and of one governor who was a part of it from the start.

Seeking Consensus on Education Goals

When he took over as chairman of the National Governors' Association (NGA) in the summer of 1989, Iowa Republican Governor Terry Branstad's Consensus for Change agenda included an education plank. He asked then-Governor Bill Clinton and me to co-chair an NGA task force charged with setting national goals for American education. At that time, President George Bush also announced his intention to call the nation's governors together for a summit meeting, whose sole topic was to be education. NGA persuaded the Administration that the summit should focus on the need to establish national education goals, rather than on programmatic initiatives.

In preparation for the summit in August and September, the NGA Education Task Force held national meetings on the need for and possible uses of national education goals, hearing from the whole range of education stakeholders. While support for the concept of goals seemed strong, there were always as many different visions of what the final product would look like as there were people in the hearing room. Yet there were broad areas of agreement: the importance of accountability based on results, the need to be sensitive to equity issues, the importance of focusing not just on the college-bound, the need for explicit links between the school and the needs of the work place, and the importance for our goals to reflect international realities.

There also was agreement that the goals should be lifelong. While Branstad originally envisioned the goals focusing on the traditional public school years of kindergarten through high school, it became clear that the seeds of educational success are planted long before a child first steps into a classroom: success today depends on personal educational growth continuing formally or informally long after high school or college graduation. National goals must reflect the realities of the 1990s. As one who completed a college education while serving in the United States House of Representatives, I was especially convinced that America's education goals must be lifelong.

The Charlottesville Summit

In late September of 1989, Hurricane Hugo struck South Carolina. The state was devastated; lives were lost; property damage was staggering. Yet barely more than a week later, I traveled to Charlottesville, Virginia, for the historic education summit held by President Bush and the nation's governors. I did so, even in the face of the pressing needs at home, because the work we were embarking on in Charlottesville — to remake education in this century — seemed to me to be nearly as urgent and critical a recovery effort as the hurricane cleanup. Both would affect the future of my state; both would help shape its economy. It was a mission no governor could afford to ignore.

At Charlottesville, President Bush and 49 governors reached agreement. We would set and be bound by ambitious national education goals that would challenge every learner in America to new, higher levels of performance. Moreover, we agreed that the governors and the President would take responsibility for seeing that progress toward the goals would be measured; and we agreed to be accountable, ourselves, for the success or failure of the effort.

As governors, we made a commitment to undertake major state-by-state efforts to restructure our education systems. In turn, we challenged the Administration and Congress to make regulatory and legislative changes to provide greater flexibility and enhanced accountability in the use of federal resources.

It sounds as though it should have been an easy agreement to reach. But getting there meant that we had to frame a process by which we could arrive at a fair and workable balance between equity and excellence — an enormous challenge. We had to decide how the federal government, which is not responsible for education in the same way as the states, could accept accountability. We had to define the principles that would guide us. The task was far from simple.

The session in Charlottesville lasted into the early morning hours. At the table were Governors Branstad and Clinton, White House Domestic Policy Advisor Roger Porter, and me — along with Ray Scheppach and Michael Cohen of the Governors' Association. We talked through the areas of agreement, argued over the language of the "communiqué" we would release, and pushed each other to make progress. And we did make progress.

Based on the principles established at Charlottesville, the NGA Task Force went back to work to flesh out the goals themselves. The Task Force held hearings and consulted with experts and practitioners. Many governors held education summits in their own states. By early 1990, we agreed on six performance goals and 21 objectives related to them. The six goals explicitly endorsed by the governors and the President state that by the year 2000:

- All children in America will start school ready to learn.
- The high school graduation rate will increase to at least 90%.
- American students will leave grades 4, 8, and 12 having demonstrated competency in challenging subject matter, including English, mathematics, science, history, and geography; and every school in America will ensure that all students learn to use their minds well, so they may be prepared for responsible citizenship, further learning, and productive employment in our modern economy.
- U.S. students will be first in the world in science and mathematics achievement.
- Every adult American will be literate and will possess the knowledge and skills necessary to compete in a global economy and exercise the rights and responsibilities of citizenship.

- Every school in America will be free of drugs and violence and will offer a disciplined environment conducive to learning.

Setting the goals — clear and ambitious improvement targets relevant to all Americans from the early childhood years through adulthood — was the first element in the National Education Goals process. Setting a deadline — the year 2000 — to achieve the goals challenges our society to be ready for the demands of the next century.

The National Education Goals Panel

Once the goals were in place, the governors turned to the question of how best to monitor national progress. Given that the task force co-chairs were from Arkansas and South Carolina (both smaller, poorer, more demographically diverse states with histories of below-average scores on national standardized tests) it is not surprising that we wanted to look beyond the simple "wall chart" mentality that pitted state against state, without regard to underlying causes. Instead, we looked for a process that would measure performance against high national standards and focus on a state's improvement from year to year.

The governors were adamant that the goals process not be federalized. To say the least, we felt strongly about maintaining a strong state influence over the process. We also believed that we needed a politically accountable process that would be responsive to public concern in the event of federal intrusion. Others, however, felt that the process should be in the hands of education professionals — that politicians were not competent to oversee highly technical measurement issues. As the governors convened for our annual meeting in Mobile, Alabama, in the summer of 1990, Democrats in Congress also raised concerns about their lack of involvement in the process.

In Mobile, emotions ran high and matters got out of hand rather quickly. Finally, after a highly unusual series of private meetings between governors and Roger Porter (representing the President), creation of the National Education Goals Panel was proposed. Colorado Governor Roy Romer, a Democrat, was named its first chair; and he presided over the birth of one of the strangest hybrids in the history of American government. An unprecedented bipartisan association of governors, senior Administration officials, and non-voting congressional representatives, this panel was charged with monitoring and reporting annually to the American people on the progress made by the nation and by each individual state toward achieving the education goals.

The panel was legitimized by an executive order of the President and by a National Governors' Association policy statement and funded by the good will, first, of the Bush Administration and then by the Clinton Administration. In many ways, the panel was actively opposed by Congress, which felt no ownership and resented the non-voting status of the congressional members. In a peacemaking effort when I chaired the goals panel during its second year, I sought and achieved a change in the NGA policy and the President's executive order, giving four members of Congress full voting rights, so that today they are active participants in the process.

An important and unusual characteristic of the panel is the willingness of the principals to devote both time and staff to its work. There is no proxy voting on the goals panel. Not only do the principals themselves participate in panel meetings, but the work leading up to its meetings is done by the goals panel staff in close consultation with the members' personal staffs. This protects the panel's political sensitivity.

The goals process would have faltered by now if the goals panel had been configured differently. Its membership represents the range of political opinion in America, and its decisions are respectful of concerns on both the right and the left. Yet the fact that the members are policy makers who are used to making tough calls enables the panel to take some politically risky, yet eminently sensible, positions. The panel has been the driving force toward high national academic standards; an important contributor to the debate on how best to measure the readiness of young children for school; a strong supporter of the National Assessment of Educational Progress (NAEP), which tells us how America's students are performing; a promoter of the need to assess what students learn in college; and a consistent voice for the importance of placing educational emphasis on performance, not simply on dollars or other inputs. Its decisions have not always been popular, but they have generally been forward-thinking and wise.

The goals panel will issue its fourth annual report in September 1994, on the anniversary of the Education Summit. The panel has now been authorized and expanded by Congress, which has somewhat redefined its role. This has made its future secure; time will tell what the changes will do to its relevance and courage.

The Role of Congress

When he chaired the goals panel, Governor Romer spent many days on Capitol Hill trying to gather support for the panel and the goals process. Despite those efforts, to this day many in Congress who are in positions of influence over national education policy remain unfriendly to the panel. From the beginning there has been tension — particularly but not solely from Democrats in the House of Representatives — over the appropriate role for Congress.

Initially, the National Governors' Association viewed the goals primarily as a state-centered project. However, the Charlottesville Summit and the resulting partnership between President Bush and the governors significantly raised the visibility of the effort and thus changed the stakes. The National Education Goals became the centerpiece of national education policy. Congress, quite understandably, wanted to be involved.

Fairly early on in the process, in late 1989, the White House convened a meeting to try to bring together the congressional education leadership, Administration officials, and governors around the goals. It was a disaster, partly because scheduling difficulties precluded the Democratic governors from being represented. Members of Congress derided state efforts; and White House officials nixed in no uncertain terms the prospect of another national meeting, which some of the congressional group had hoped to arrange.

Tensions escalated when members of Congress were denied full voting rights on the goals panel. But the reason for that decision was very simple: Members of Congress do not run programs and hence cannot be held directly accountable for the results of education policy. The governors had no desire to alienate Congress. But the partnership created at the Charlottesville Summit was based on the willingness of governors and the President to take public responsibility for measurable progress in reaching the education goals. We were having a hard enough time trying to figure out how to hold the executive branch accountable for results in an environment that had never before measured anything but inputs. We simply did not see a way to extend that accountability to Congress.

Moreover, the governors already were skittish about ceding any influence over education goals and standards to the federal government, even as full participants and in partnership with an Administration that we believed shared our confidence in the states as the appropriate governance level for education policy. Our experience with Congress suggests that once it is invited in, Congress finds it hard to contribute without wanting to control.

Several members of Congress were particularly interested in and informed about aspects of the goals process. Senator Jeff Bingaman

(D-N.M.), in particular, was knowledgeable about the outcomes focus of the goals and the importance of high national standards against which performance-based goals could be measured. He was the author of early legislation in this area. Likewise, Congressman Bill Goodling (R-Pa.), ranking Republican on the House Education and Labor Committee, had written into law a provision calling for a national meeting on education, much like the Charlottesville Summit but with a broader array of participants. Early on, Congressman Goodling recognized the importance of national buy-in if education reform is to be successful.

The Standards Council

The first test in working with Congress on the goals process came through our experience with the National Council on Education Standards and Testing (known as NCEST). Once again, I was tapped to co-chair, this time with Governor Romer, who had shown real leadership in the standards movement during his chairmanship of the goals panel.

The panel already had convened a working group on national standards headed by Lauren Resnick of the University of Pittsburgh, a recognized national expert in the standards area. Her group had recommended that the nation proceed with establishing internationally competitive standards in the core academic subjects identified in the goals, and the panel had endorsed her report. The new Education Secretary, former Tennessee Governor Lamar Alexander, who sat on the panel, was willing to engage the resources at his command to support the development of national standards. So the train was already on the track.

Because of concerns over the implications of national standards, NCEST was authorized by Congress and charged to: 1) advise on the desirability and feasibility of national standards and tests; and 2) recommend long-term policies, structures, and mechanisms for setting voluntary education standards and planning an appropriate system of tests.

Membership on the council was broad and diverse, and included members of Congress, state legislators, education stakeholders (including officials from state departments of education and testing specialists), business people, and representatives of the Administration, as well as the two governor co-chairs.

The controversy over national standards was and is generated by the specter of a national curriculum dictated by the federal government. The governors and many other elected leaders oppose a national curriculum. National standards should specify only the basic academic understandings that all students need to acquire. They were never meant to dictate everything a student should learn. This is why the goals themselves specify core subjects and why there is resistance to adding additional goals.

Throughout its deliberations, the council found that the absence of explicit national standards, keyed to world-class levels of performance, severely impairs our ability to monitor the nation's progress toward the National Education Goals. Historically, we have evaluated student and system performance largely through measures that tell us how many students are above or below average or that compare relative performance among schools, districts, or states. Most measurements cannot tell us whether students are actually acquiring the skills and knowledge that they will need to prosper in the future. They cannot tell us how good is "good enough."

As Governor Romer and I pointed out in our introduction to the NCEST report, in the absence of well-defined and demanding standards, education in the United States has gravitated toward de facto minimum expectations, with curricula focusing on low-level reading and arithmetic skills and on small amounts of factual material in other content areas. Most current assessment methods reinforce the emphasis on these low-level skills and on processing bits of information, rather than emphasizing problem solving and critical thinking. The adoption of world-class standards would force the nation to confront the disturbing reality that our performance expectations for education are simply too low.

During its deliberations, the council flirted with the idea of including "school delivery" or "opportunity-to-learn" standards as an element of the national standards system. The arguments are compelling on the surface: No one believes that a student should be held to a high standard in the absence of the tools that would make high achievement possible. The question is, Who makes the decision on what tools are necessary and appropriate or, conversely, that the opportunities provided are inadequate? Should it be parents, teachers, and the local district, or should it be Washington?

Unfortunately, I came late to the debate. I had unavoidably missed the two NCEST meetings where the issue of nationally defined "school delivery" standards was raised. I am not insensitive to this issue. As an example, when we examined the causes for low math SAT scores in South Carolina, we found that the kids who had access to the courses were doing okay; but many of our children did not even have access to appropriate courses. When we responded to that need, we found scores improving. However, all of my experience indicates that the schools that perform best are the schools that have the flexibility to respond to the needs of their students. If students are achieving at high levels, why should the state or the federal government step in? Only when students are not achieving should outside action be considered; and even then such action should be tailored to the needs of the individual schools, not prescribed by some state or federal formula. Problems are best solved by the people closest to them; they are seldom solved by fiat from Washington.

In the end, the council came to that conclusion. In keeping with the notion that states and communities should be given as much flexibility as possible, the council defined "school delivery" standards as standards that would be developed by the states collectively, from which each state could select the criteria that it finds useful for the purpose of assessing a school's capacity and performance. It rejected the notion of "one size fits all" input standards for the nation's schools, and embraced yet again the principle that at the national level the focus should be on performance targets, with states given wide latitude to design the conditions under which those targets would be achieved.

The council released its report in January 1992. It endorsed the concept of standards and a voluntary national system of assessments, but it did so with very specific stipulations. According to the report, the standards must:

- Reflect high expectations, not expectations of minimal competency.
- Provide focus and direction, not become a national curriculum.
- Be national, not federal.
- Be voluntary, not mandated by the federal government.
- Be dynamic, not static.

The report also stipulated that the system of assessments must:

- Consist of multiple methods of measuring progress, not just one test.
- Be voluntary, not mandatory.
- Be developmental, not static.

The other major controversy addressed by NCEST concerned governance. How were the standards and the system of assessments to be put in place? In hindsight, two of the most contentious issues surrounding the goals have had to do with process: first, setting up the goals panel itself and, second, working out its relationship with a new standards council. Given the sensitivity about where the controls over education and curriculum are located, I guess that's not really so surprising.

One of the most controversial aspects of the council's deliberations concerned the method by which oversight of new national academic standards would be shared between a standards council, dominated by the education establishment, and the politically accountable goals panel. The compromise was worked out largely by the staffs of the co-chairs and our congressional membership — Senator Bingaman, Senator Orrin Hatch (R-Utah), Congressman Dale Kildee (D-Mich.) and Congressman Goodling. This compromise tied the panel and a new National Education Standards and Improvement Council (NESIC) together inexorably. The goals panel would appoint members of NESIC from specific categories, including public officials, educators, and the general public. Standards or assessments could be approved only with affirmative action by both bodies.

Goals 2000: The Educate America Act

Even before the standards council report was released in early 1992, governors' staff began negotiating with the staffs of Senator Bingaman and Secretary Alexander to translate the report into legislative language. Although they had participated in the NCEST negotiations, staffs of the House members had not felt comfortable committing their principals to the governance structure that had now been agreed on. So they were not at the table at this point.

In 1992, the bill (then called the Neighborhood School Improvement Act) passed both houses of Congress and nearly made its way out of a House-Senate conference committee. However, controversies concerning school choice, opportunity-to-learn standards, and the role of the goals panel finally scuttled the effort for the 102nd Congress.

When Bill Clinton was elected to the presidency, most observers believed that the goals and standards movement would be in good hands. Clinton was one of the fathers of the goals and seemed certain to protect the integrity of the process. When he named Dick Riley, former governor of South Carolina, as Secretary of Education, it seemed even more likely that the Administration would give scrupulous attention to the need to preserve state and local control over the end uses of goals and standards.

But the reviews are mixed.

The Clinton White House has received its share of criticism for its inability to deal effectively with the Congress. Nowhere has the lack of

87

legislative savvy been more clearly demonstrated than in the debate over the Goals 2000 legislation. Look at it this way: Here was a bill that Congress had been working on for several years. It nearly passed during the Bush Administration. With a Democratic President dealing with a Congress controlled by Democrats, it should have been easy. Yet Goals 2000 took nearly a year and a half to enact.

Because of my position in the leadership of the National Governors' Association, I was a close observer of the congressional process, although I was not a participant. Since the substance of the legislation is detailed elsewhere in this book, I will focus only on gubernatorial reaction to a process that seemed chaotic from the start.

The governors expected to enthusiastically support Goals 2000, particularly since one of its main objectives was to give us some flexibility in the use of federal education funds. As it was initially presented to governors' staffs, however, the Administration bill was fatally flawed in three ways. First, it tinkered with the membership, duties, and ground rules for the goals panel enough to subvert the panel's character as a high-level, voluntary partnership leading the nation in striving to achieve the National Education Goals and world-class standards. Control over the education standards process was ceded totally to a new council likely to be dominated by the very education establishment that had been so reluctant to be held accountable.

Second, though we envisioned states being able to receive some sort of "seal of approval" for their education assessments, the bill provided procedures for states to seek approval not only for their assessments, but for content and opportunity-to-learn standards. Our model would have allowed for approval of state assessment instruments that reflected high national standards; but state content standards (essentially state curricula), and certainly opportunity-to-learn standards, were not to be federally approved. As noted earlier, many governors — and I was one — strongly objected to federal prescription either of what students should learn or the conditions under which they should learn.

Third and most ominous, the bill was presented as the Administration's framework for future legislation and funding. There were strong indications that this portended the tying of future federal education funding to federally approved state standards.

The governors at that point threatened to walk away from the process. We were shocked by the course of events, particularly because the very people involved in writing this legislation were those who had been at the table when the goals process was first initiated. After intense negotiations, the Administration agreed to seek changes in the bill from the House Committee on Education and Labor, which was to consider the legislation first.

From the outset, the Democrats in the House were most hostile to the flexibility inherent in the goals process. The Senate and Republicans, in general, were friendlier to the concepts embodied in the goals. The Clinton Administration's attitude toward the course of events in the House struck me as curious. It seemed cowed by the Democrats on the Education and Labor Committee and preoccupied with getting a bill — any bill — out of committee and to the floor. Not surprisingly, the House version of the Goals 2000 bill was unacceptable to governors and opposed by the NGA.

At the request of the Administration, which promised to work with us later in the legislative process, we focused our lobbying on the Senate version of the bill, which was much more acceptable to governors. The Senate bill, as it went to the floor, struck an acceptable balance between the respective roles of the goals panel and the new standards council and included more appropriate language on opportunity-to-learn standards.

However, several aspects of the Senate bill needed clarification before NGA felt that it could fully support the measure. We asked for and received several amendments, in particular one that would specify in the bill itself the voluntary nature of state content, performance, and opportunity-to-learn standards and prohibit mandating certification of these standards as a condition for state participation in any federal education programs. The conference between the House and Senate to resolve differences in the bill reportedly was brutal. The most contentious issues were the problems that the governors had identified. I was deeply concerned, particularly about the opportunity-to-learn issues and, based on our early work on the goals, wrote President Clinton a personal letter expressing that concern. In response, the President wrote:

> Because I believe so strongly that every child can learn, I believe that actual student performance is the best measure of the extent to which equal opportunity to receive a world-class education has in fact been achieved. . . . As the House/Senate conference proceeds, my representatives have been directed to work hard for a final bill that reflects our long-standing commitment to the National Education Goals, to historic state and local prerogatives in education, and to bipartisan cooperation. As a key element of that effort, I have instructed Administration representatives to support language on opportunity-to-learn issues in Goals 2000 consistent with the principles and framework of the Senate bill.

NGA's lobbyist on education issues, Patricia Sullivan, worked effectively and made a great deal of progress in hammering out acceptable compromises. In particular, she and the Senate staff did an excellent job with the language on opportunity-to-learn standards, which requires states to develop — although not necessarily implement — standards or strategies for providing all students with a fair opportunity to achieve the knowledge and skills described in the state's content and performance standards.

In spite of strong support from our Senate goals panel members, we were not able to work out acceptable language on the governance structure. In that section, House provisions generally prevailed. For the governors, this was a problem serious enough to persuade us to withhold unequivocal NGA support, although we did not actively oppose passage. While there have been representations that our action was partisan or politically motivated, that argument simply does not stand up against the facts.

One State's Experience: Education Reform in South Carolina

No discussion of the national efforts to establish goals and performance-based education would be complete unless it set those efforts in the context of what was actually going on in education reform at the time. In the years we spent dickering over the appropriate membership of a national standards council, real reform was already occurring out in the states.

Even before the National Education Goals, South Carolina had set goals of its own through 1989 legislation called Target 2000: School Reform for the Next Decade. The Target 2000 goals were aimed primarily at children's school readiness, reducing high school dropout rates, and raising student performance levels beyond the basic skills. These goals anticipate the ones that would be set the following year by President Bush and the nation's governors.

Like the national education goals, the Target 2000 goals gave us a framework from which to begin to build coherent education policy aimed at excellence, not mediocrity. But we quickly discovered — as the nation was to discover — that our progress could be only halting and piecemeal until some other important building blocks had been put into place.

The first obstacle we faced was that South Carolina had never developed standards that would explicitly state what we want our kids to know and be able to do — not just for now, but for the new century in which these kids will live and work.

90

Without such content standards, our goals were meaningless. Why measure student progress if what kids were learning was not what they needed to know?

To address this problem, South Carolina now has developed standards — called curriculum frameworks — in three subjects (math, foreign languages, and art), with five more on the way. The curriculum frameworks are closely aligned with the national standards now under development in the core subjects and serve the same purposes, to define the body of skills and knowledge to be attained in each discipline and to suggest how that body of skills and knowledge can best be communicated from teacher to learner.

South Carolina's first three frameworks, developed with the direct input of 3,200 educators, business representatives, and members of the general public, are explicit attempts to focus all instruction, curriculum, assessment, professional development, and classroom materials on the levels and kinds of skills graduates will need to lead productive lives. The math framework, for example, emphasizes sophisticated analysis and interpretation of real-life problems. The foreign language framework calls for high-level competency in daily communication skills and for early and sustained foreign language instruction for all students.

But having standards doesn't guarantee higher achievement. Again, there were other building blocks that had to be put in place before we could expect to see the effects of our reforms. In particular, once we had new, higher standards, we also would need new ways of measuring achievement against them. Our old basic-skills tests were geared to minimum performance and, therefore, were useless in assessing skills at higher levels.

In response to that need, in 1990 the Governor's Task Force on Educational Accountability was established to review the state's assessment system and recommend changes that would bring it into line with the new goals and standards. Legislation embodying the Task Force's recommendations and calling for a comprehensive overhaul of the state's testing practices has garnered strong support in our General Assembly and is expected to pass in the next session.

When it does, South Carolina will have put in place — on its own initiative and sometimes in advance of any guidance from the national or federal level — many of the essential elements on which the national education goals process is based. The state will have agreed-on goals; it will have challenging standards; it will have an assessment system capable of measuring performance at high levels and providing accountability based on results.

And it will be an education system that recognizes the benefits of providing flexibility in return for proven performance. In South Carolina, that flexibility has been extended to schools through two sweeping legislative reforms: The Target 2000 Act and the Early Childhood Development and Academic Assistance Act. In contrast to the highly prescriptive reform bills of the 1980s, one of the explicit purposes of the Target 2000 legislation was to free already high-achieving schools from the straitjacket of state regulation and to allow them to build the programs and operating procedures that seemed, in their own judgment, most likely to take their students to the next level of success. Schools that met certain performance criteria were exempted from state law and regulations governing the basic skills testing program and the remedial and compensatory education program, as well as from state dictates concerning such matters as the organization of the school day and year, staffing patterns at the school level, and class size. Qualifying schools remain in the program so long as they continue to meet the accountability criteria specified in the law.

Since 1989, when the act was passed, 283 schools have been deregulated under these provisions. In addition, 130 schools were awarded three-year grants under the act to encourage them to develop innovative programming. Thus Target 2000 was a significant first step toward a new kind of accountability in education policy, one that relies not on top-down regulation, but rather on giving schools both the freedom and the financial incentives they need to establish "break the mold" programs.

The Early Childhood Development and Academic Assistance Act, passed by the General Assembly in 1993 and generally referred to as Act 135, took South Carolina another long stride down the road toward results-based local empowerment and decision making. The statute, which is aimed both at front-end prevention of learning problems and at keeping students on track as they move through school, is considered to be at least as sweeping in its scope as the state's landmark Education Improvement Act (EIA) of 1984.

Act 135 reallocates almost $100 million of state education funding to help prepare children for the first grade and to ensure that the classroom experience is challenging for all students. To accomplish those objectives, the legislation radically re-orients the state remedial and compensatory program to provide high-quality, short-term, intensive help to low achievers, in place of the watered-down curriculum and poor teaching that have typically been offered to students who fall behind.

Where Target 2000 represented important evolutionary change — it kept the individual EIA programs intact but built new reforms on top of them — Act 135 is revolutionary in the sense that it encourages schools and districts to completely rethink the ways in which they organize and deliver services. Where the EIA's remedial and compensatory program dictated to schools and districts which students must be served, for how long, and through what means, Act 135 encourages local communities — that is, schools acting in concert with parents, community leaders, and others — to make their own decisions about which students need help and how and when that help should be provided.

The latitude extended to communities in making those decisions is wide. They can use the state's dollars either for special academic assistance to students who are having learning problems or for a range of other interventions — some of them entirely outside the normal K-12 enterprise, such as parenting classes or programs for three- and four-year-olds — designed to prevent problems from developing in the first place. In designing the approaches they will use, schools and districts (again, acting with parent and community input) are directed to develop plans that include performance goals and that integrate the planning and direction of all programs to meet those goals.

Building on the limited grant-based program established in Target 2000, Act 135 provides special innovation funding to all schools and districts to encourage them to find entirely new ways to promote high-quality teaching and learning. And the Act calls for a focus on results through state-level assessments at the end of grades three and eight and through the exit exam.

In its education reform initiatives, South Carolina has adhered closely to the fundamental philosophy behind the national goals process: challenging standards for all students, an orientation toward results, maximum flexibility in return for maximum performance, decision making at the level closest to the problem, and a high degree of parent and community involvement. All of these reforms were initiated in advance of the federal passage of Goals 2000 through the entirely voluntary action of a state that recognized the value of the principles on which the goals process was based. They are typical of the kind of creativity, the thinking "outside the lines" with which states across the country already have responded to the challenges that process puts before them.

Furthermore, states in the vanguard of reform have taken seriously not only the principles behind the goals process, but the goals themselves. In South Carolina, the national education goals have helped particularly to sharpen the focus of the policy debate in the areas of school readiness (Goal One), standards and assessments (Goal Three), mathematics and science (Goal Four), and adult literacy and workforce preparedness (Goal Five). In each of those areas, the state has given high priority to the issue and has taken substantive action that will assist in meeting the goal.

In the area of school readiness, for example, South Carolina has undertaken a multi-pronged effort that crosses health, human services, and education lines to provide children with a firm foundation for learning before and during their early years in school. Act 135, the Early Childhood Development and Academic Assistance Act, is central to that effort, providing for statewide parenting and family literacy training, expansion of child development programs, increased funding for special academic assistance to children in grades K-3, a required planning process to draw together all state and federal resources and programs in early childhood, and cooperative efforts among health, human services, and education providers.

In addition, two recent initiatives testify to the state's success in addressing issues of access to health care for children and their mothers — an important factor in school readiness. Caring for Tomorrow's Children, a unique public-private venture that provides incentives in the form of coupon books for various products and services for early and continuous pre-natal care, has so far served 145,000 pregnant women in the state, most of them from low-income households. A campaign initiated by the governor's office in 1993 to immunize children age two and under has already exceeded its current 80% target and promises to meet or exceed its 90% goal for next year. Taken together with other ongoing cabinet-level initiatives targeted at teen pregnancy, improving the quality of state-funded child care, and family preservation, these programs hold real promise for bettering the conditions in which children begin their lives and their learning careers.

With regard to the fourth national education goal — first-in-the-world status in math and science achievement by the year 2000 — South Carolina already has put in place the mechanisms for ensuring that instruction in those disciplines will be world-class. The Governor's School for Science and Mathematics, a two-year residential program established as one of the first initiatives of my administration, provides advanced training at no cost to the state's top students. In 1992, the school was named one of the best in the nation by *Redbook* magazine, testifying to the extremely high quality of its academic program.

Simultaneously, South Carolina is engaged in a massive statewide drive to re-train teachers in the new curriculum frameworks and new assessments in math and science already developed or under development in the state. This initiative, funded by a grant of almost $10 million from the National Science Foundation and organized explicitly around Goal Four, establishes a network of regional centers, or "hubs," to make training and technical assistance available within easy driving distance for every teacher in the state.

Each hub is organized and operated by a local board with representation from all participating school districts and institutions of higher education, the business community, and other civic representatives. State-level oversight and direction is provided by the Governor's Mathematics and Sciences Advisory Board, a broad cross-section of policy makers, business people, and math and science leaders. The high degree of active participation in the initiative not only by educators but by others outside the education arena (particularly business representatives, who now chair not only the state-level board but five of the local boards) signifies a strong consensus on the future shape and direction of reform in math and science education.

All 13 hubs will be fully operational by the summer of 1995. By 1998, an estimated 7,000 teachers and 1,400 administrators will have participated in the training institutes and other activities of the hubs, substantially affecting the quality of teaching in classrooms across the state.

Finally, South Carolina has given much attention to the problems of adult illiteracy and poor worker preparation that are addressed by Goal Five. In part, it was South Carolina's experience that inspired me to insist that the goals be lifelong in nature and for all learners, not just for children. The Governor's Initiative for Work Force Excellence, a program established in the second year of my administration to help workers upgrade their skills through job-related training, now serves more than 400 companies and has trained some 20,000 individuals statewide. The initiative, now considered a national model, has proven extremely successful as a strategy for returning adult workers to the classroom and helping to engage them in the kind of lifelong learning called for in the goal.

At the same time, the state has recognized that the best worker training programs begin with the acquisition of appropriate skills in elementary and secondary school and with efforts to link classroom learning to real-life jobs. To meet those needs, I have just signed the School-to-Work Transition Act, which recognizes for the first time that South Carolina must give as much priority to the education of students bound for early careers as to those bound for the college campus.

The legislation, supported not only by the governors' office, the State Superintendent of Education, and the legislative leadership but also by a coalition of education and business groups, will significantly raise performance expectations by eliminating the high school general track in favor of a rigorous, structured sequence of courses designed to provide strong academic as well as technical preparation. In addition, to help students meet marketplace demands, the act calls for incorporating statistics, logic, measurement, and probability into the mathematics sequence and for including other skills and competencies identified by industry as important for on-the-job success.

To assist students in making the transition from school to work, the act requires career counseling in cooperation with parents, beginning as early as kindergarten. It also encourages mentoring, apprenticeship programs, and other local initiatives to help students connect with employers and work-based training opportunities even before they graduate from school. Like Act 135 on readiness, to which this statute is tied through the school and district planning process, the School-to-Work Transition Act asks educators to engage in a thorough, thoughtful redesign of the ways in which they serve students — especially those students traditionally relegated to the unchallenging bottom rung of the education ladder.

Clearly, in its education reform effort, South Carolina has framed a policy agenda that responds directly to the national education goals. The goals have been written into law by the General Assembly and endorsed both by the state's agency heads for health, human services, and education and by the Business-Education Partnership for Excellence in Education, a state-funded, blue-ribbon committee for education policy.

No federal mandate could have produced the outpouring of public interest, debate, and support that accompanied publication of the state's first curriculum frameworks; no mandate could have persuaded the South Carolina legislature to pass Target 2000 or Act 135 or the School-to-Work Transition Act. These steps, all of them radical departures from previous practice, were taken because the state recognized the legitimacy of the issues raised by the goals and determined to seek answers.

And in the end — in a lesson that has profound implications not only for the future of federal education policy but also for the relationships between states and their schools and between teachers and their students — the answers that South Carolina found on its own initiative were far more creative, more thoughtful, and more far-reaching than any that could have been envisioned or prescribed by Capitol Hill. It is a lesson we should all take to heart.

What's Next?

Some have argued that the national education goals are unrealistic and irrelevant. But five years later, nearly all the states have adopted goals based on our national work; and Congress has endorsed them, albeit with a few additions. As readers can see from what has happened in South Carolina, the very way we think about education is changing.

There are others who say that by adopting the goals, we opened a Pandora's box of undue federal intrusion and inappropriate standards dealing with values and morals. Some states have made mistakes and have had to pull back because of legitimate concern about the appropriate role of government at any level in our children's education. As one who has spent quite a lot of time dealing with these issues — as co-chair of the initial NGA task force, as a member of the Education Goals Panel for three years and its second chairman, as co-chair of the National Council on Standards and Testing, and finally as vice-chair and chairman of the National Governors' Association — I think both schools of thought have some validity. The jury's still out.

What I do know is that it is critical for governors from both parties to keep a close eye on the goals and standards movement. We are the ones who gave it life, and we are the only ones who can keep it on track.

Washington Post editor Dave Broder in a recent editorial called the idea of national education goals "a truly radical notion" and nationally defined competency standards and tests "even more radical." He wrote that agreement on these ideas came from the governors who, he said, understood that "seeking consensus did not mean making only small plans."

Today, there are only 15 sitting governors who were at the Education Summit in Charlottesville, and that number will be reduced to a maximum of 7 after the 1994 elections. Nevertheless, at an extraordinary private session at a recent National Governors' Association meeting, governors of both parties talked frankly and knowledgeably about the national education goals, the Goals 2000 legislation, and development of standards at the national level. It is clear that governors — Democrat and Republican alike — share a deep concern about the implications of national goals and standards, particularly with respect to undue federal influence over education and the possible development of non-academic standards or a national curriculum. But, after all the talking was done, it is just as clear that today's governors remain committed to the principles we articulated when the goals process started and are determined to keep the process on the right track.

Systemic Reform and Goals 2000

By Jennifer O'Day

Jennifer O'Day is associate director of the Pew Forum on Education Reform at Stanford University. She has written extensively on systemic reform strategies and issues.

Jennifer O'Day's current research interests include the effects of reform policies on traditionally underserved students and issues of teacher and system capacity for systemic reform.

With the passage of the Goals 2000: Educate America Act, Congress has set the stage for a new national role in support of education improvement. Central to this new role are the codification of the National Education Goals (Title I) and the authorization of voluntary national content, performance, and opportunity-to-learn standards (Title II). Taken by themselves, these titles represent an unprecedented step. But Goals 2000 goes beyond either rhetoric or standard-setting by authorizing federal monies to states for comprehensive reform of their education systems (Title III). This support for systemic improvement in the states represents a significant shift in federal education policy, one motivated by a growing perception that fundamental educational change is not only desirable but necessary to the economic, social, and political well-being of the nation.

The purpose of this chapter is to outline the concept of systemic reform underlying the design of Goals 2000, to provide a few examples of what states already are doing to systemically reform their education systems, and to discuss how Goals 2000 might assist in these efforts.

What Is Systemic Education Reform?

As the term *systemic reform* has come into popular use in the past few years, it has taken on a variety of meanings depending on the context and the users. By systemic reform, some mean multiple improvement efforts pulled together into a comprehensive — though not necessarily coherent — package. To others the term implies efforts to broaden the "system" to include comprehensive children's services as well as school learning. There also are those who use *systemic reform* interchangeably with *school-based restructuring*, while still others take it to mean simply a combination of student standards and related assessments.

The concept of systemic reform undergirding Goals 2000 focuses on improved student learning through clear, common standards and coherent policy support for school-based change. The intent of such a strategy is to combine the vitality and creativity of bottom-up change efforts with an enabling and supportive structure at more centralized levels of the system. In an earlier paper, Smith and O'Day (1991) identified three interconnected aspects of this concept of systemic reform: 1) unifying vision and goals, including a core of ambitious learning outcomes for all students; 2) coherent instructional policies aligned in support of achieving that vision; and 3) a restructured system of governance and resource allocation that places greatest authority and discretion for instructional decisions on those closest to the students — that is, teachers and others at the school site.

Unifying vision. At the heart of systemic reform strategies is the contention that the fundamental change sought by reformers and public leaders will not occur without a clear and agreed-on vision of the schooling we desire for all children. This vision, based on an understanding of the central purposes and goals of education, would provide the direction for a coherent and sustained public and professional effort toward their realization. Content and performance standards will embody much of that vision by articulating what we expect young people to know and be able to do at various points in their schooling and when they enter the workforce or higher education.

It is important to note that the standards envisioned by Goals 2000 (both state and national) differ from previous standard-setting in this country in two critical ways. First, they are to embody *high* expectations and *challenging* content, placing emphasis on depth of understanding, effective communication, and an ability to grapple thoughtfully with novel and complex problems. These are skills many observers regard as necessary for productive and responsible citizenship in our diverse society. As such, they stand in sharp contrast to the basic skills and minimum competencies of the 1970s and early 1980s, which set baseline or threshold levels of acceptable performance. Developed through a broad participatory process, the proposed standards would balance the professional judgment of scholars and educators about what constitutes challenging and meaningful material with what many individuals and groups believe is important for our young people to learn.

A second difference between this effort and previous efforts is the view that these ambitious standards should apply to *all* students — that is, all children should have access to the new challenging content and, moreover, should be expected to learn it to a high level of performance. Simple justice dictates that this should be the case; if certain knowledge and skills are deemed necessary for productive citizenship, they must be available to all future citizens. This argument is bolstered by recent psychological theory and research that finds all children capable of complex thinking and high levels of accomplishment when given the chance (for example, Resnick 1988). If the knowledge and skills are valued and necessary and if virtually all children are capable of acquiring them, then schools have an obligation to provide all students the opportunity to do so. (See O'Day and Smith 1993 for a fuller treatment of equity issues and strategies in systemic reform.)

These twin concepts of high expectations and equal opportunity form the cornerstone of systemic reform strategies. Commitment to their realization is articulated in statements such as Delaware's "Excellence and Equity for All" or Vermont's "Very high skills for every student, no exceptions, no excuses." It also is the basis for the opportunity-to-learn standards and strategies called for in Goals 2000. These strategies will be designed to help ensure the fiscal, material, and human resources necessary to move slogans like these from rhetoric to committed action.

A coherent and supportive policy structure. One advantage of a clear vision is that policies can be designed to work together to reinforce that vision. The state policy components most often targeted for alignment with the standards include curriculum frameworks, textbook adoption criteria, teacher education, student assessment, and accountability. Consistency and coherence among these elements could function in two ways to reinforce and sustain instructional reform at the school level.

First, such alignment could result in consistent signals being sent to schools about what is important for teachers to teach and for students to learn. Such consistency is a far cry from the way education systems function today. Currently decisions about education are influenced by a myriad of actors and agencies at all levels inside and outside the system, each with its own goals, interests, and timetables. The resulting policy fragmentation pulls teachers in multiple and often conflicting directions, as when adopted curricula stress one set of student outcomes and tests used for student and teacher accountability assess an entirely different set.

Fragmentation also squanders precious resources and diverts attention away from the core mission of teaching and learning. Time is wasted on meaningless bureaucratic compliance while both public and private monies disappear into ineffective programs or the latest fad.

The second benefit of policy coherence is that it targets resources where they are most needed and most effective in fostering the desired outcomes. For example, monies for professional development could be spent on activities that actually enhance teachers' ability to teach the content of the standards, rather than on disconnected courses or ineffective one-shot workshops. In addition, states can leverage the development of instructional materials that support students' learning the standards, thus freeing teachers from the burden many now face of either adapting poorly suited texts to the new learning goals or creating the needed materials from scratch. One example of this is California's use of textbook adoption criteria that reflect the state's curriculum standards. Because state monies can be used only for approved texts, districts have an incentive to use and publishers have an incentive to create texts and other materials that are consistent with the standards.

Assessments in such a system would be designed to provide useful information about how the student or the system was progressing in achieving the standards. This is unlike the current standardized tests, which are purposefully disconnected from the content of instruction and thus of little value to teachers or students. By contrast, results from new standards-based assessments could be invaluable both for tailoring instruction to particular students' needs and for evaluating and improving educational practice.

Aligning new policies with the standards will not be enough, of course. Contradictory policies will have to be eliminated and the entire structure made leaner, cleaner, and more supportive of local practice. At the same time, the state may need to develop additional strategies to provide resources, build capacity, and increase motivation for school-based change.

Restructured governance. Because of the emphasis on standards and on state policy coherence, many observers assume that systemic reform is a top-down strategy focused on centralized decisions with standardized implementation at the local level. Such an interpretation is not surprising given the current bureaucratic nature of the system, but it is not the strategy envisioned by the designers of Goals 2000. Nor is such an interpretation likely to lead to the kinds of changes in instruction or stu-

102

dent learning desired (Fuhrman et al. 1988; Sarason 1990; Darling-Hammond 1993).

The starting point for systemic reform strategies is an understanding that improvements in school learning can happen only where such learning occurs — *at the school* through interactions of students with students, students with educators, educators with other educators, and the entire school with the community. Thus at the center of the strategy — equal in importance to the notion of policy coherence — is the view that the school must be the focal point of change and must have the resources, flexibility, and authority to effect that change. Moreover, it is with those closest to instruction — the teachers — that most of this authority should rest.

The value of placing greater authority and discretion in the hands of school personnel is supported by research on organizational effectiveness. Non-school research finds that control over work tasks and opportunity to participate in making decisions increase worker commitment and motivation (Firestone and Pennell 1993) and system productivity (Lawler 1986; Blinder 1990). Moreover, high involvement of workers is especially beneficial where the work is complex, is best done collegially, and exists in a rapidly changing environment. These conditions all apply to education (Mohrman et al. 1992), particularly in an era of reform and changing demographics.

The reform emphasis on teaching for deep understanding underscores the need for a high degree of school-site discretion and for policies that support professional communities in and beyond the school (Cohen et al. 1993). New conceptions of learning place the student at the center as meaning is negotiated and built, rather than conveyed. The teacher, in this conception of learning, becomes a facilitator of the knowledge construction process, a role that requires not only deep understanding of the content and of pedagogy but also sufficient flexibility and control over resources to use that knowledge to respond to the needs of students. Finally, the ability of individual teachers to function in this way is enhanced when all the teachers at the school are able to collaborate in developing a coherent mission, in designing curriculum and allocating resources to promote that mission, and in increasing their knowledge base (Purkey and Smith 1983; McLaughlin 1993).

Using the Top to Support the Bottom

At this point, one might ask: If school authority and discretion are so important, why not just leave schools alone to develop the best instruc-

103

tional programs for their students? Why all this emphasis on policy? Indeed, there are many reformers who believe that school-based change and centralized direction are incompatible. They argue for a school-by-school strategy of reform that relies on networks of schools, rather than policy structure, to lend coherence and support.

As appealing as such an approach might be, several factors make it unpromising as a means for accomplishing ambitious outcomes for all students. One is that schools do not exist in a vacuum, and the effects of the fragmented system continue to be felt even when schools manage to buffer themselves through waivers, charter arrangements, or other strategies. Moreover, a side-effect of the current fragmentation is that even very successful schools generally lack an external support system that can help them maintain their success over a long period of time — including appropriate materials from which to choose, a pool of knowledgeable and committed teachers, high-quality professional development, and adequate assessments. Networks among schools can help and may be a necessary part of any successful school reform strategy. But these networks cannot provide the infrastructure, much less the resources, needed to overcome inevitable problems of burnout, personnel turnover, or shifting policies.

Nor do they provide sufficient basis for generalizing instructional improvement reforms beyond a small number of already reform-minded schools and teachers. The equity implications of this are substantial. Because schools with large numbers of currently underserved poor and minority students face additional problems that drain their energies, resources, and attention, they are generally the least likely to benefit from school-by-school strategies (O'Day and Smith 1993).

Finally, the type of teaching and learning implied by many of the proposed reforms not only is very demanding but also is something to which relatively few teachers have been exposed, either in their own experience as students or in their professional preparation and inservice programs. Thus achieving it will require considerable development of teachers' knowledge, as well as changes in beliefs and practices. Like any complex change, this is a very difficult process. It will not happen unless and until teachers see alternatives to what they have always known and done — and until they have the chance to examine, experiment with, and reflect on the alternatives over a period of time (Cohen et al. 1993)

Coherent state and local policy can provide such opportunities by creating an environment in which change is expected and encouraged; in which the direction of change is consistently and concretely expressed through standards, assessments, and professional development; and in which teachers are drawn into activities that allow them to experience and reflect on new approaches to teaching and learning. In many ways this kind of policy environment is parallel to the kind of learning environments many reformers are asking teachers to create in their classrooms. Putting students at the center of the learning process does not negate the role of the teacher; it transforms that role into one of facilitator and coach. Similarly, putting the school at the center of reform does not negate the role of district and state policy. Rather, it transforms it into one of facilitating and guiding teacher learning and school change.

Examples of State Systemic Reform

Unified vision, coherent policy, restructured governance — there is a logic to their combination. But is all this really possible? Can states and communities agree on learning goals and a vision to guide instruction? Will the bureaucracy allow schools the necessary freedom? Will instructional guidance stifle creativity or unleash it? Are we asking schools and teachers to do too much?

A number of states are in the process of experimenting to find answers to these questions. Following are brief descriptions of three such states — California, Vermont, and Kentucky — each of which began its reform efforts well before the Goals 2000 legislation.

California's systemic reform efforts began as early as 1983, when then-State Superintendent of Public Instruction Bill Honig secured the passage of Senate Bill 813, an omnibus reform bill that included among its 65 components model curriculum standards, textbook adoption criteria, expansion of the California Assessment Program (CAP) — now the California Learning Assessment System (CLAS) — and the establishment of the School Improvement Program (SIP).

At the heart of the strategy are subject-based curriculum frameworks, developed and revised in staggered seven-year cycles. The frameworks are designed to be conceptual road maps, focusing on the big ideas in each field and in many cases taking decisive stands on new or controversial issues, such as process approaches to writing instruction or teaching about religion in history (Massell 1994). The frameworks provide guidance on *what* to teach — generally in large four-year blocks — but not on *how* to teach. Although they are not mandatory, they have become the basis for coordinated assessment, textbooks, and other instructionally related policies and incentives.

Several aspects of the California strategy are worth noting. One is the heavy reliance on professionals for the development of the curriculum frameworks, including university professors, teachers, professional organizations, and other educators with subject-matter expertise. As a result, the frameworks are based on each discipline instead of being interdisciplinary. They also reflect reform ideas in the content of each field and new conceptions of the way children learn. On the one hand, this process has added to the coherence in general philosophy among the frameworks, making them mutually reinforcing. On the other, because they represent the "state of the art," California frameworks and the newly developed state assessments differ significantly from the experience of most teachers and the general public, which creates obstacles to acceptance and implementation.

Second, the central role of the frameworks developed over a ten-year period as they influenced textbook adoption, assessment, and the work of the California Subject Matter Projects and others involved in the professional development of teachers (Kirst and Yee 1994). Several school-based strategies have been added or revised to support the reform goals. These include networks of elementary, middle, and high schools. These networks are based on broad reform documents that are intended to assist participating schools in pulling together the various pieces of reform into a coherent whole at the school level. State restructuring grants also have been allocated on a competitive basis to selected schools, while the broader School Improvement Program has revised its program quality review to engage schools in more self-study.

Finally, while the effects of the reforms on instruction are beginning to be seen in a number of schools, teacher and school capacity is a major issue (Cohen et al. 1994). And in a time of deep recession and mushrooming student enrollment in the state, the fiscal, demographic, and political challenges are severe.

A continent away from California, Vermont differs in both conditions and strategy. A small state with a comparably homogeneous population and long tradition of local control, Vermont bases reform not on any single piece of comprehensive legislation but on a set of conceptually linked initiatives that have been developed primarily in the past five years. Also, Vermont's overall strategy is more populist in process and less discipline-based in outcome than the California effort (Massell 1994).

At the center is *The Vermont Common Core of Learning* (1993), which was developed through broad public discussion in focus forums conducted in various regions of the state. In these forums people were asked open-ended questions about what Vermont children should know and be able to do. The result was a set of broad competencies called "vital results," organized into four groups: communication, reasoning and problem solving, personal development, and social responsibility. The *Common Core*, which remains in draft form, was opened for public and professional discussion and comment. More content-based standards now are being added — though in broad fields rather than disciplines — and they will be cross-referenced to the vital results in a forthcoming draft. Also included are core principles of learning, teaching, and assessment that help to define the overall vision of education in the state.

Another important piece of the Vermont reform is the statewide portfolio assessment in grades four and eight. The assessment is performance-based; it builds on the common core competencies; and it has involved widespread teacher participation, becoming an avenue for teacher professional development consistent with the learning goals. Vermont's generally populist approach also has been evident in the portfolio development; when independent evaluators raised questions and criticisms, these were aired publicly and the assessments were revised. A standards board also was created in 1989 to link teacher competencies to the frameworks.

Perhaps the most comprehensive of any state systemic reform effort, Kentucky's model illustrates yet another approach. The catalyst for the Kentucky effort was a landmark court ruling in 1988, which directed the state legislature to create a system that would provide a "free and adequate education to all students throughout the state" (*Council for Better Education* v. *Wilkinson,* No. 85-CI-1759, Franklin Cir. Ct., 14 Oct. 1988). In 1990 the General Assembly passed the comprehensive Kentucky Education Reform Act, which contains several key strategies, including goals and outcome accountability combined with school-based management, linkages between schools and other children's services through Family Resource Centers, and extended school services to assist at-risk students.

Like Vermont, Kentucky had a public discussion of goals that led to competency and skill-based outcomes in the form of six broad goals, initially, which then served as the basis for 75 "valued outcomes." These outcomes recently have been incorporated into a large comprehensive curriculum framework covering language arts, math, and science.

Several aspects of Kentucky's strategy are important to note. One is the comprehensive nature of the reform effort, encompassing preschool and out-of-school factors as well as content, school structure, and governance. A second is the emphasis on outcome accountability, with rewards and sanctions to go to schools based on results on student assessments. Third, because of the short timeline for the accountability system, the assessments actually preceded the development of the frameworks or professional development. Finally, unlike either California or Vermont, the Kentucky reform mandated school-based management throughout the state, although the interpretation of how roles and responsibilities should be defined varies among the districts.

These state examples have common threads. For example, all three states have or are developing student standards to define the goals of instruction. Yet they differ in the process by which these standards have been developed (specifically in the balance between professional and public input), the form of the standards (broad competencies and interdisciplinary approaches versus discipline-based frameworks), and in the other goals brought into the reform vision, such as comprehensive children's services.

Each state also is working to establish coherence among its policies, most notably by developing assessments that reflect the desired outcomes and by establishing professional development activities that better prepare teachers to help their students reach them. However, there are variations in the timelines and in the dominant policy instrument (assessments versus frameworks), in additional policies affecting curriculum (such as California's emphasis on criteria for textbook approval), and in the avenues for professional development.

Finally, all three states have addressed governance and school-based strategies; but Kentucky stands alone in the extent to which it mandates school-based management and accountability for improved student performance.

These three states, of course, are only three examples among the many states instituting more coherent reform strategies; and they do not reflect the full range of strategies chosen. They do provide evidence, however, that Goals 2000 enters into a play that is already in motion. The question is, how will this new national legislation advance the play and what are the potential problems with its implementation?

Assistance for State Systemic Reform

Goals 2000 provides both symbolic and concrete support for systemic improvement efforts like those described. Symbolically, the act lends legitimacy to standards-based reform, both through its authorization of voluntary national standards and through its delineation of the components that states should include in their systemic improvement plans. It underscores the need for standards to apply to all students' performance and calls for the development of strategies to ensure that all students have an adequate opportunity to learn. It emphasizes the need to redefine roles and responsibilities throughout the system so that decisions regarding instruction are made by those closest to the students. And it emphasizes the importance of community involvement and teacher professional development.

Goals 2000 also includes several kinds of concrete support for state reform efforts, including monetary grants to states and, through the states, to localities and teacher education and professional development consortia. This fiscal support will help many states whose reform efforts are under-funded and jeopardized by economic recession and inadequate state budgets. In addition, the development of national standards will provide useful models for states that have limited capacity or are just beginning the standard-setting process. Finally, the linkage of Goals 2000 with other federal legislation, in particular the reauthorized Elementary and Secondary Education Act, paves the way for more efficient and effective uses of federal assistance to help poor and special needs students meet the standards.

Beyond these symbolic and concrete supports, Goals 2000 provides a model on a national level of many of the kinds of strategies suggested for states. It begins with a general statement of goals (vision) and establishes a process for the certification of the voluntary national standards. This process includes the establishment of broadly representative, nongovernmental bodies: the National Education Goals Panel (NEGP) and the National Education Standards and Improvement Council (NESIC). These are similar to the state panels called for in Title III. The act also is non-prescriptive, providing guidance for the state plans but leaving considerable room for variation. And it allows for waivers from certain federal statutory and regulatory requirements if they impede the ability of the state or locality to carry out the improvement plan.

The bill's bipartisan passage and broad support among education groups are an example of the sort of political consensus-building that will be necessary in the states if they are to develop and implement coherent plans. Perhaps most important, Goals 2000 lays the conceptual groundwork for other federal legislation, establishing a model for coherence among federal and national endeavors in education that has never been seen before and may help states achieve similar coherence among their reform initiatives.

A Few Concluding Cautions

Despite the promise of systemic reform, many tensions and potential pitfalls might prevent the realization of its very ambitious goals. Some observers have identified important implementation issues that have arisen in state efforts to date, and I would direct the reader to more complete discussions. (See, for example, Fuhrman and Massell 1992.) In the following paragraphs, I draw attention to four issues that I believe will affect the implementation of Goals 2000 and state reform efforts.

Standards alone do not a vision make. Throughout this chapter and in much of the current reform literature, "vision" and "standards" are used almost interchangeably. This may be a mistake.

No matter how well-articulated a statement of desired student outcomes may be, by itself it will not lead to a coherent strategy for their attainment. Indeed, our vision must go beyond the development of common standards to an articulated and agreed-on concept of the type of system and schools that will help all children attain high outcomes. This vision must reflect the values, understandings, and conditions of each state or locality and serve as the basis for policy design and school improvement strategies. Without broad articulation, we are unlikely to move beyond business as usual and the results that current practice already produces.

Consider, for example, one aspect of such a vision: the conception of teachers and teaching. I have suggested in this chapter that if we are to develop complex thinkers and problems solvers, teachers must be developed and supported as professionals with deep knowledge and problem-solving skills, responsibility for instructional decisions, and a commitment to personal learning. This view of the teacher as a professional has important implications for the type of policies we might develop to achieve the standards. For example, it implies greater commitment of time and resources to continuing professional development, the design of preservice and professional development opportunities that are rooted in practice and that encourage reflection and collaboration, and a greater reliance on professional judgment for curriculum development, assessment, resource allocation, and school improvement. By contrast, a view of teacher as technician, far more common in our education culture, leads to quite different policies involving standardization, compliance with set procedures, and bureaucratic control.

My point here is not to argue that teacher professionalism must be part of the larger vision, though I believe it must. Rather it is to stress that the elaboration and articulation of such principles must be a deliberate and public part of the standard-setting and reform process. Reform does not take place in a vacuum. Our schools are steeped in a culture, a factory model of schooling that is bolstered both by the classroom experience of most adults (including teachers) and an almost impermeable bureaucracy. If we wish to really change what happens in classrooms and schools, we must change that culture — slowly, consciously, consistently. Otherwise, new practices will be drowned out, marginalized, and eventually obliterated by old habits. And the old system will reinvent itself on the ashes of the new.

Another reason for clear and public articulation and agreement on principles is that public understanding, involvement, and support are essential if the reforms are to take hold. We already are seeing the emergence of considerable confusion in many localities and states, misgivings and even fear of new approaches to education. Most misgivings arise from misleading messages that distort the intentions and nature of the reforms, but they also arise because average Americans are too little involved in the development of reform goals and strategies. When involvement does occur, as in the case of Vermont, we see greater public patience in solving problems and greater general public support.

Variation: Accept it, value it. Despite its logic, many unresolvable tensions and questions are inherent in systemic reform. Examples include the tension between common standards and the diverse needs, backgrounds, and interests of students and teachers; the tension between the "top" (centralized guidance) and the "bottom" (decentralized practice); the tension between subject knowledge and interdisciplinary problems and competencies; the tension between attention to process and attention to content. States and localities will balance these tensions differently, depending on their particular histories and conditions. Each higher level in the bureaucratic system must accept variation in levels below and use that variation to learn more about the effectiveness of various practices. Systemic strategies and new approaches to teaching and learning have very small databases at present. We can use the variation in implementation to learn more about what works and what does not.

This inevitable variation raises several questions for the implementation of Goals 2000. For example, how will NESIC handle varying approaches to standards and disagreements among disciplinary experts? Will it certify one or more sets of standards in each subject area? How will the secretary evaluate state plans? What is the acceptable degree of variation in kinds of student outcomes or in opportunity-to-learn goals and strategies? Answers to these and related questions imply choices along the standardization/variation continuum, and they should be made with careful attention to their potential consequences.

Think capacity! Given a vision, the capacity to do the work necessary to realize that vision is critical. Perhaps one of the most consistent lessons from current state reform efforts is the need to focus on building the capacity to accomplish the reform goals.

Three types of capacity needs come to mind. One is resources — of all kinds. Another is the development of organizational structures that not only allow but encourage and support practices that lead to improved learning. And a third is developing the requisite knowledge in individuals responsible for instructionally related work so they can effectively carry out that work. Such development includes professional development of teachers, of course, but also developing learning opportunities for school administrators, district personnel, and state department of education personnel. These individuals not only must learn about the relevant content in their field but also must learn about how to carry out the new roles that restructuring their institutions implies.

Such knowledge development is largely a state issue, but the federal government can play an important role by drawing attention to the need for capacity building, popularizing effective strategies for addressing capacity issues, and assisting SEAs in developing their own capacity to lead and carry out systemic improvement.

The fourth dimension: Time. Throughout this chapter I have referred to three aspects of standards-based systemic reform, each of which involves fundamental changes. These are creating a unified vision, developing coherent policy to support it, and restructuring governance to facilitate change. However, my recent interviews with California teachers, along with the work of other researchers, have led me to believe that there may be a fourth dimension along which fundamental transformations must occur. This fourth area of change concerns our use — indeed, our very conceptions — of *time.*

On one level the needed change is obvious and already in motion. Prescriptive requirements that chop up student learning time into predetermined, static, and unrelated segments thwart efforts to probe deeply into subject matter, to coordinate across disciplines, or to respond to student learning needs. Accountability based on student learning rather than seat time may allow schools to move away from such requirements. But this is only the beginning.

Equally problematic is the allocation of teachers' time. The demands for teacher learning and for responsiveness to student progress suggest a need for increased time in teachers' work schedules for collaborative planning and reflection. Some observers have gone so far as to suggest that half of a teacher's work day should be devoted to such activities, as is the case in some other industrialized nations. Underlying such suggestions is a radically different view of teacher effectiveness as related to instructional time, one that deserves investigation.

Perhaps most relevant to Goals 2000 and standards-based reform is the need to rethink our conceptions of a timeline for systemwide change. Even if all teachers had the requisite knowledge and even if high-quality standards and assessments were already developed, it would take years to see deep changes in teachers' practices and perhaps much longer to see substantial improvements in student learning. But such preconditions are not present.

Many teachers do not have the requisite knowledge. In most states, standards and assessments (much less instructional materials, strategies, and professional development) are just in the beginning stages of development. Under these conditions, national and state leaders must be especially careful about how they define progress toward the reform goals. To promise substantial near-term improvements in student learning, for example, may produce the temporary support needed to pass legislation but then doom the long-term effort when dramatic student achievement gains are not immediately realized.

The situation is further complicated by the uncertainty inherent in our endeavor. Indeed, in systemic reform we are embarking on a journey for which there is no clear map. We have an idea of where we are headed. But like all explorers, we are charting the terrain as we go. To discover the best paths will require experimentation, risk taking — and time. We need policies that can keep us moving forward but that allow for and encourage the exploration necessary to find our way.

To this end, the federal government might do well to assist states in developing interim indicators of improved practice so that accountability needs can be addressed without thwarting local initiative or creating disillusionment. Similarly, the Secretary and those charged with evaluating Goals 2000 will need to develop criteria that take into account existing capacities and the complexities of systemwide reform. Finally, the federal government and other interested parties might lend considerable support by providing resources for school-based research and by popularizing promising practices and progress along the way.

Such progress does exist. In states and school districts across the country there are exciting examples of restructuring schools, of educators working collectively to design and institute new approaches to curriculum and assessment, and of policy attempts to spread these reforms to previously untouched schools and teachers. Particularly encouraging are recent data indicating that instructional reforms are seeping into increasing numbers of typical schools, even those enrolling large numbers of disadvantaged children (Cohen et al. 1994). Perhaps if we learn to recognize and to track such indicators of progress, they will become our signposts along the road to the kinds of challenging student outcomes that the standards describe and that the American people want.

References

Blinder, Alan. *Paying for Productivity.* Washington, D.C.: Brookings Institute, 1990.

Cohen, David K.; Barnes, Carol; Mattson, Steve; Poppink, Sue; and Price, Jeremy. "The Progress of Instructional Reform in Schools for Disadvantaged Children." Paper presented at the Annual Meeting of the American Educational Research Association, New Orleans, 1994.

Cohen, David K.; McLaughlin, Milbrey W.; and Talbert, Joan. *Teaching for Understanding: Challenges for Policy and Practice.* San Francisco: Jossey-Bass, 1993.

Darling-Hammond, Linda. "Reframing the School Reform Agenda: Developing Capacity for School Transformation." *Phi Delta Kappan* 74 (June 1993): 753-61.

Firestone, William A., and Pennell, James R. "Teacher Commitment, Working Conditions, and Differential Incentive Policies." *Review of Educational Research* 63, no. 4 (1993): 489-525.

Fuhrman, Susan H.; Clune, William H.; and Elmore, Richard F. "Research on Education Reform: Lessons on the Implementation of Policy." *Teachers College Record* 90, no. 2 (1988): 237-57.

Fuhrman, Susan H., and Massell, Diane. *Issues and Strategies in Systemic Reform.* New Brunswick, N.J.: Rutgers University, Consortium for Policy Research in Education, 1992.

Kirst, Michael W., and Yee, Gary. "An Examination of the Evolution of California State Educational Reform, 1983-1993." In *Ten Years of State Education Reform, 1983-1993: Overview with Four Case Studies,* edited by Diane Massell et al. New Brunswick, N.J.: Rutgers University, Consortium for Policy Research in Education, 1994.

Lawler, Edward E., III. *High-Involvement Management.* San Francisco: Jossey-Bass, 1986.

Massell, Diane. "Achieving Consensus: Setting the Agenda for State Curriculum Reform." In *The Governance of Curriculum,* edited by Richard F. Elmore and Susan H. Fuhrman. Alexandria, Va.: Association for Supervision and Curriculum Development, 1994.

McLaughlin, Milbrey W. "What Matters Most in Teachers' Workplace Context?" In *Teachers' Work: Individuals, Colleagues, and Contexts,* edited by Judith W. Little and Milbrey W. McLaughlin. New York: Teachers College Press, 1993.

Mohrman, Susan A.; Lawler, Edward E., III; and Mohrman, Alan M., Jr. "Applying Employee Involvement in Schools." *Educational Evaluation and Policy Analysis* 14, no. 4 (1992): 347-60.

O'Day, Jennifer A., and Smith, Marshall S. "Systemic School Reform and Educational Opportunity." In *Designing Coherent Education Policy: Improving the System*, edited by Susan H. Fuhrman. San Francisco: Jossey-Bass, 1993.

Purkey, Stuart, and Smith, Marshall S. "Effective Schools: A Review." *The Elementary School Journal* 83, no. 4 (1983): 427-52.

Resnick, Lauren B. *Education and Learning to Think*. Washington, D.C.: National Academy Press, 1988.

Sarason, Seymour B. *The Predictable Failure of Educational Reform*. San Francisco: Jossey-Bass, 1990.

Smith, Marshall S., and O'Day, Jennifer A. "Systemic School Reform." In *The Politics of Curriculum and Testing*, edited by Susan H. Fuhrman and Betty Malen. Philadelphia: Falmer, 1991.

The Vermont Common Core of Learning: Education for the 21st Century. Montpelier: Vermont Department of Education, 1993.

PART II
SCHOOL TO WORK

Building a Framework for a School-to-Work Opportunities System

By Robert B. Reich
Secretary of Labor

Robert B. Reich is the nation's 22nd Secretary of Labor. Prior to his appointment by President Clinton, he was on the faculty of the Harvard University John F. Kennedy School of Government.

Secretary Reich served as an assistant to the Solicitor General during the Ford Administration, and he headed the policy planning staff of the Federal Trade Commission during the Carter Administration.

Secretary Reich graduated from Dartmouth College and Yale Law School. He also received a degree from Oxford University, where he studied as a Rhodes Scholar. He is the author of seven books and numerous articles on the global economy and the U.S. workforce.

On 4 May 1994, only 15 months into his Administration, President Clinton signed into law the School-to-Work Opportunities Act. The new law represents a down payment on a commitment to help Americans adapt to the dramatic economic changes occurring all over the world. As governor, Bill Clinton had witnessed the deteriorating economic prospects of non-college-educated youth. As President, he was determined to change this course.

The School-to-Work Opportunities Act is both an ending and a beginning. It is the culmination of many years of thought and study about how to prepare young people for academic and occupational advancement; it is the start of a new journey by the many partners who will be involved in addressing these challenges.

The legislation also represents a critical step toward closing a gap in this country's workforce development system. The United States is the only major industrialized country that has not had a comprehensive and coherent system for providing young people with the tools they need to make the transition from school to a first job with a good future. And the absence of a coherent system has produced devastating results for too many youth and for the American economy as a whole.

Fortunately, a number of forces have converged to bring about change. Demands have come from many arenas, including employers dissatisfied with the poor quality of entry-level workers and educators and parents who have seen students floundering in high school and dropping out or graduating with little ability to build a sustainable career.

President and Mrs. Clinton were among the many Americans who entered the debate from years of involvement with education reform and with a deep awareness of the need to improve the way young people are prepared for the workforce. They were joined by many others, in both parties, who believed that it was time to address this important issue. The impact of this legislation has yet to be felt. But the commitment of a broad spectrum of individuals to bring about a school-to-work system — a commitment that crystallized in the legislation but that now extends beyond it — portends meaningful change in how this nation educates youth and thus strengthens our economic health and ability to complete.

The Need for a School-to-Work Transition System

During the 1980s evidence accumulated that the American education system was failing to meet the needs of non-college-bound students. Several indicators appeared: a widening earnings gap between workers who are well-educated and those who are not; the many years spent moving in and out of low-wage, low-skill jobs for youth with only a high school diploma; and the lack of any employment for many inner-city minority youth.

Public awareness of these problems rose between 1987 and 1990, when two widely disseminated reports were published: *The Forgotten Half* and *America's Choice: High Skills or Low Wages*. In many important ways these reports became a catalyst for policy proposals.

The gap between the average income of college graduates (who constitute only a quarter of the U.S. working population) and everyone else doubled during the 1980s and continues to widen. The real wages of the young and less-educated plummeted, breaking the historic pattern of rising earnings for American workers at all skill levels. In the early 1990s the real hourly pay of recent male high school graduates was more than 20% below that of their counterparts 20 years earlier. The decline in pay of high school dropouts has been even more extreme.

The days when high school graduates could expect to move directly into well-paying factory jobs are over. Expanding global trade and investment have forced Americans to compete with people around the world, many of whom are willing to work for less. New technologies in manufacturing and, increasingly, in services are shrinking the demand for and undermining the earning power of unskilled labor.

Neither of these forces can (or should) be kept at bay; on balance, they make the nation richer. But as low-skill, high-paying jobs disappear, more workers without college degrees are finding their wages, benefits, and living conditions declining. As the Clinton Administration took office in January 1993, there was a broad-based awareness that America must do a better job of equipping our citizens to prosper in this rapidly changing global economy. In particular, we needed to address two phenomena:

- the lack of a comprehensive system to prepare youth for high-skill, high-wage jobs; and
- the shift in demand toward workers with skills and away from workers without them.

The *America's Choice: High Skills or Low Wages* report observed that "America may have the worst school-to-work transition system of any advanced industrial country." Countries such as Germany, Japan, Singapore, Sweden, and Denmark were ahead of the United States in offering young people a smooth transition from school to working life. In these countries, but not in the United States:

- Virtually all students reach a high educational standard.
- "Professionalized" education is provided to non-college-educated workers to prepare them for their occupations and to ease their school-to-work transition.
- Comprehensive labor market systems are operated that combine training, labor-market information, job search, and income maintenance for the unemployed.
- Company-based training is supported through general revenue or payroll tax-based financing schemes.

Youth in these countries graduate from high school with significant occupational skill training and are prepared to enter the labor market.

Because of this, employers are willing and eager to hire young people out of high school.

In contrast, American schools generally are designed to prepare students for college, not work. High schools typically have strong ties with colleges and weak ties with employers. Yet three-fourths of high school students will enter the workforce without college degrees. Too many of these young people also leave high school without basic academic or occupational skills and without adequate preparation for work or for further education. In this country, only one large firm in 10 hires new high school graduates, according to a recent survey.

High school graduates who do not go to college frequently spend five to ten years in the "youth labor market," typified by low wages, low benefits, and low security. While some youth will work their way out of this process into the adult labor market, research done by Paul Osterman at the Massachusetts Institute of Technology shows that "as many as 50% of high school youth had not found a steady job by the time they reached their late twenties."

Youth who live in impoverished urban and rural communities around the country face even greater challenges. Labor market shifts have hit disadvantaged young males especially hard. The real wages of young, less-educated males have fallen dramatically over the past quarter-century. The nonemployment rate for 20- to 24-year-old nonwhite males increased from 22% in 1964 to 42% in 1992.

The Foundation

For a decade or more, national, state, and local policy makers and program operators, academicians, foundations, and interest groups have labored to lay the groundwork for a national school-to-work initiative. There has been much debate on the proper federal role. During that time a number of bills authored by both Democrats and Republicans (including Senators Kennedy, Simon, Breaux, Jeffords, Hatfield, Thurmond, and Hatch and Representatives Gephardt, McCurdy, Goodling, and Gunderson) were introduced in the Congress. States such as Arkansas, Maine, Wisconsin, Georgia, and Oregon enacted their own school-to-work legislation. The federal Department of Labor funded youth apprenticeship demonstration projects. All of this activity was important for synthesizing core themes, formulating options, and reaching a consensus on the key features for national legislation.

The so-called youth apprenticeship model (inspired by a number of the European training systems) attracted considerable attention. Imple-

122

menting a youth apprenticeship program in Arkansas was one of Bill Clinton's significant achievements as governor. A national expansion of this approach was one of his commitments to the American people during his campaign for the presidency.

The growing number of youth apprenticeship programs link school and work by integrating academic instruction with work-based learning and work experience. In addition to teaching skills for a specific job and general "employability skills," youth apprenticeship aims to affirm academic learning and to demonstrate its link with the workplace. Adult mentors guide students' experiences on the job, and students often rotate from job to job to obtain a broad view of related occupations and skills. Successful youth apprenticeship programs have strong employer involvement. Many provide a certificate of occupational skills mastery. And generally the student receives a wage paid by the employer.

Although youth apprenticeship programs contained most of the essential features of a school-to-work transition system, there were issues that had to be addressed in the policy development process.

First, labor unions were committed to preserving the integrity of traditional registered apprenticeship and preferred its expansion over the creation of a separate youth apprenticeship system. Unions were concerned about the risk of substituting youth apprentices for current workers, lowering labor standards, and possible duplication of current apprenticeship programs and erosion of the quality of basic education.

Second, youth apprenticeship programs were small in number. Fewer than 4,000 students were enrolled in youth apprenticeship programs in 1993. Furthermore, youth apprenticeship was by no means the only game in town. Important expertise and resources for a school-to-work transition system existed in this country's vocational education community and the expanding network of community colleges and technical schools.

For example, amendments to the Carl D. Perkins Vocational and Applied Technology Act in 1986 and 1990 were designed to strengthen vocational education programs by emphasizing the integration of academic and vocational curricula, as well as the acquisition of general skills and a broad array of knowledge in all aspects of an industry. Of particular note was the Tech Prep program, created in the 1990 reauthorization of the Perkins Act. Tech Prep is designed to link the last two years of high school with two years of college or technical school in a progressive curriculum that leads to an associate degree.

Ultimately the school-to-work initiative drew inspiration not only from the youth apprenticeship model but also from a number of other innovative school-to-work transition programs. Safeguards also were built into the initiative's design to prevent any displacement of existing workers or lowering of labor standards.

As we thought through the questions of how to build a school-to-work system, we knew we needed the advice and expertise of businesses, labor unions, education groups, state and local governments, community-based organizations, and others. In fact, we hoped that we could form an effective working partnership, not unlike the partnership that we knew was essential for any truly workable state or local school-to-work program. And in the end, these groups played a major role in developing the school-to-work effort. The full range of our constituencies came together. And, since new federal funding was being authorized for this legislation, no group felt that another program was being diminished.

One partner was absolutely essential — the U.S. Congress — and we wanted to work closely with those congressional leaders, Chairmen Bill Ford and Ted Kennedy among others, who already had demonstrated leadership on this issue. In the end, that partnership, perhaps more than any other, made the difference.

Developing School-to-Work Legislation

Although Secretary of Education Richard Riley and I did not know precisely what the Administration's school-to-work initiative would look like, we did know that we were going to design and implement it together. The partnership has been deep and genuine, perhaps to the surprise of some Washington skeptics. Our perspectives have complemented one another. Secretary Riley and his staff often talk about this legislation in the context of secondary school reform and reinventing American high schools. I emphasize training to meet a changing economy and the need to be competitive. The legislation reflects our joint thinking.

We take pride in the two departments' collaboration on the school-to-work initiative itself as an example of reinventing government. We see our partnership being paralleled at the state and local levels by educators, employers, workers, parents, elected officials, and other interested parties.

When we started this process, we knew our challenge was to make change happen quickly and to make it happen nationwide. As we prepared the Administration's first budget, we proposed laying the groundwork for a school-to-work system with states and communities even prior to the enactment of new authorizing legislation. In a remarkable gesture of support, the appropriations committees provided funds to both departments under existing legislative authority in order to start implementation of a school-to-work system while proposed legislation was still moving through the Congress.

We knew that we had to galvanize the full array of state and local job training and education resources. New federal resources would be limited ($100 million was ultimately appropriated for our first year of implementation in FY 1994). It also was important for us to craft a new kind of bill — one that reflected the spirit of "reinventing government." It could not be a typical top-down approach. To ensure that there would be both local flexibility and nationwide consistency, we developed a number of strategies that eventually were adopted by the Congress — and that now permit rapid construction of a national system. These include:

- States will have *multiple avenues* to build school-to-work systems with federal support — through the use of 1) development grants, 2) implementation grants, and 3) waivers to provisions in existing job training and education programs. These strategies will enable faster start-up and diffusion of school-to-work systems and more flexible and creative strategies.
- The legislation provides *venture capital* for states and local communities to build a school-to-work system. Our goal is to promote ongoing community ownership of and responsibility for bettering young Americans' career and educational opportunities, but not to create another top-down permanent federal program. Funds for school-to-work will need to leverage other resources from federal, state, and local programs in order to implement and sustain a system.
- Implementation of the school-to-work system will come in "waves" — starting with the states that already are set for reform and ending with the states that are just starting this process. In this way, limited federal funds will go first to states where they can make the most difference. These more advanced states and communities also will be laboratories to generate and test new ideas.
- For states that have yet to receive implementation grants, local grants, waivers, and existing funds can be used to begin building school-to-work opportunities.
- By design, we are leaving considerable room for experimentation and local diversity. The legislation does not require adherence to

a single model. Nevertheless, there are *key unifying themes* to guide development of the new system. The legislation calls for students to receive:

a. a work-based learning experience;
b. school-based learning that provides an integrated curriculum of academic and occupational learning;
c. a high school diploma or its equivalent, enabling enrollment in college-level education; and
d. an occupational skill certificate, enabling entry into a first job on a career path.

- Key features of the youth apprenticeship approach will be integrated with other, larger programs, such as cooperative education, career academies, and Tech Prep.
- Business and labor leadership is critical to the success of all aspects of this initiative. Employers — in partnership with labor — will play a key role in the design and implementation of the system, including defining skill requirements for jobs, serving on state and local partnerships and governing bodies, offering quality work experiences for students, and providing post-program job opportunities for students and graduates.
- Finally, this initiative is designed to serve all students — a broadly inclusive group within the nation's student population, including the disadvantaged, students with disabilities, students who have dropped out, and the academically talented.

Congressional Strategy

When the Administration's bill was sent to the Congress on 4 August 1993, there was a solid base of support. The key congressional forums were the Senate Labor and Human Resources Committee and the House Education and Labor Committee. Although the Administration's bill was not considered controversial, we still anticipated negotiations and compromise.

During the development of the legislation, we conducted periodic consultations with virtually all groups that expressed an interest in the legislation. This process was invaluable. Recommendations frequently led to improvements in the drafting of the bill. Ongoing consultations helped to ensure broad-based support for the bill during its congressional consideration.

Secretary Riley and I also consulted frequently with the authorizing leadership in both chambers. We felt fortunate that we had two of the best committee chairmen to move the bill and to help us keep our coalition together. Constant communication and collaboration also took place at the staff level. We knew that the Senate Labor and Human Resources Committee and the House Education and Labor Committee had a full plate of other legislative initiatives. Nevertheless, they treated this legislation as a priority. The support and cooperation of the chairmen and their staffs were essential.

We also actively recruited bipartisan co-sponsors for the legislation. In an interview shortly after the bill was introduced, a House Democratic staff aide was asked about the Administration's proposal: "Why the love feast?" The aide replied, "The Administration has been cognizant of the work we've already done and has been able to address enough of everybody's concerns so that everybody feels it's headed in the right direction."

Secretary Riley and I also made site visits with key members of the Congress to local school-to-work programs during the developmental stages of the bill. I observed students training in such diverse occupations as metal workers at a Harley Davidson plant and as technicians in an operating room at the New England Medical Center. We saw excitement and hope in the eyes of the students. It reaffirmed for all of us the value of linking work and learning.

Both the House and the Senate moved quickly in the fall of 1993 to hold hearings and committee markups. Although each chamber made changes to the Administration's proposal, the basic elements remained intact. This reflected the initial consultations in the development of the bill and strong support by the major stakeholders.

During the House-Senate action on the bill, two significant issues emerged and would require changes before final passage: 1) a provision requiring employers to pay wages for some part of a student's work experience and 2) the question of who should be responsible for the governance of the state school-to-work opportunities system. The Administration supported paid work because it solidifies employer commitment to student workers and cuts the risk of displacing adult workers. In a compromise, the requirement of paid work experience was dropped and alternative language that *encouraged* paid experience was adopted. The governance issue was resolved through a compromise that accommodated the central role of the governor in formulating a school-to-work plan but preserved the autonomy of those state agencies not reporting to the governor.

Those issues notwithstanding, only nine months passed from the time the bill was sent to Congress to its enactment into law by the President. The House of Representatives passed the bill on 17 November 1993. Senate passage by a vote of 62 to 31 occurred on 8 February 1994. Symbolically important was Senate passage the same day of a companion measure — Goals 2000: Educate America Act. A conference committee followed quickly to resolve the outstanding issues between the two school-to-work opportunities bills. The House passed the bill 339 to 79 on April 20; the Senate followed the next day and passed the bill by voice vote. Two weeks later on May 4, the bill was signed into law.

The Connection to Goals 2000: Educate America Act

Conceptually linked to the school-to-work proposal and moving on a parallel track through the Congress was the Goals 2000: Educate America Act. Goals 2000 was passed by the Congress less than a month before the school-to-work legislation.

Goals 2000 provides a companion framework for the school-to-work opportunities system. It requires this new system to be standards-driven. It establishes a process for setting world-class academic and occupational standards for all students in school-to-work opportunities programs. Thus students will be able to complete a school-to-work program with a diploma that means something. Goals 2000 also creates a vehicle for developing occupational standards through the creation of a National Skill Standards Board. This board will identify broad occupational clusters and create a system of standards, assessment, and certification for the skills needed in each area.

American students, workers, employers, and educators must know what knowledge and skills are required in the workplace. This effort is a critical step in establishing a lifelong learning system for all Americans — for high school students, unemployed and dislocated workers, and employed workers who want to upgrade their skills. Appropriately, these two programs are being implemented hand-in-hand.

Expectations for a School-to-Work Opportunities System

The law presents a number of significant challenges for all partners, including the federal government. In the next eight years (the legislation sunsets in the year 2001), states and local communities will be able to create statewide school-to-work opportunity systems for students by:

- building partnerships among schools, employers, labor, community organizations, and parents to develop and sustain school-to-

128

work opportunity systems as part of a lifelong learning system for the nation;

- enlisting employers in providing work-based learning opportunities to young people as part of their high school experience; and
- reforming secondary schools and programs for out-of-school youth.

The goals and challenges are formidable. The Departments of Labor and Education will need to provide a new kind of leadership. This legislation offers us a test, allowing us to move the federal government beyond its traditional responsibilities toward a role as a conduit for learning.

I look forward to seeing employers compete for the students completing school-to-work programs; to seeing more productive employers as their skilled work force grows; and to the day college-prep and career-prep paths will be virtually interchangeable and have the same status with educators, counselors, parents, students, and employers. I look forward to seeing a system in which economically disadvantaged students and others with special needs achieve the same successes as other students.

I believe we have put in place the system to make this happen. Resources and time may be limited, but the commitment to succeed is not.

Establishing the Framework for "Hire" Education in America

By Senator Paul Simon

Paul Simon, a Democrat, is the senior senator from Illinois. He is a well-known writer and former newspaper editor and publisher.

Prior to his election to the U.S. Senate, Senator Simon served in the U.S. Army in the early 1950s; was elected to the Illinois House of Representatives, where he served four terms, followed by two terms in the Illinois Senate; and in 1968 was elected lieutenant governor of Illinois.

Senator Simon was elected to the U.S. House of Representatives in 1974 and served five terms before being elected to the U.S. Senate in 1984.

There is nothing more important to the future of this nation than how we prepare our young people for employment and productive citizenship. For too long we have failed to provide many of our young people with the opportunities they need to be economically self-sufficient. According to the U.S. Census Report, 20% of American children live in poverty. The Children's Defense Fund in its report, *The State of American Children*, outlines the hardships endured by impoverished children. The report urges policy makers to "leave no child behind" and focuses attention on the need to provide these young people with a chance to escape from poverty.[1]

Perhaps the greatest inequity in our society is our inability to offer equal opportunity to the poor through our public school system. In his book *Savage Inequalities*, Jonathan Kozol poignantly illustrates the seemingly insurmountable odds faced by children who grow up in poverty. They live in dilapidated housing, have insufficient health care, and struggle merely to survive in dangerous neighborhoods. They hunger not only for nourishment, but for an opportunity to succeed.[2]

In one passage of *Savage Inequalities*, Kozol quotes Father Michael Doyle, pastor of Sacred Heart Church in North Camden, New Jersey. Father Doyle poetically describes a young girl's struggle to remain optimistic:

> Still there is this longing, in this persistent hunger. People look for beauty even in the midst of ugliness. "It rains on my city," said an eight-year-old I know, "but I see rainbows in the puddles." It moved me very much to hear that from a child. But you have to ask yourself: How long will this child look for rainbows?[3]

Without opportunities to succeed, many young people are condemned to lives of hopelessness and despair. We need to encourage them to continue to look for the rainbows. However, without the skills necessary for gaining employment, many of these young people are thrust into a destructive cycle of dead-end jobs, unemployment, and welfare.

Without hope, all too many turn to lives of crime. More than 80% of those in prison are high school dropouts, and approximately three-fourths of prison inmates are functionally illiterate and lack basic skills. The correlation is undeniable. People without hope inevitably are drawn into lives of public dependency or worse — crime. We should heed the adage, "An ounce of prevention is worth a pound of cure." As a society, we seem all too willing to build new prisons and impose harsher punishment, but we seem to lack the will to invest in prevention.

Last year I held a hearing on equalizing school financing in East St. Louis, Illinois, described in *Savage Inequalities* as an example of a community with desperately inadequate education funding. In addition to hearing moving testimony from students who, tragically, have received the message from our society that we do not hold high expectations for their future or value them equally with their peers in neighboring communities, I toured a dilapidated high school. I noticed a new building being constructed down the street and was dismayed to learn that it will be a new jail.

One way we can begin to provide young people with an opportunity to succeed is to strengthen the link between school and employment. In 1987 the William T. Grant Foundation issued a report called, *The Forgotten Half: Pathways to Success for America's Youth and Young Families*.[4] *The Forgotten Half* clearly outlines our fundamental failure to help young people make the transition from school to employment, a failure also documented by Lester Thurow, who calls this "the missing middle in U.S. education."[5] About half of our students never go to college, and about half of those who do never obtain college degrees.

Young people who do go on to pursue postsecondary education often receive significant public and private aid, but those who do not go to college generally receive little help. The federal government offers aid and loans to college students and assists in funding the college and university research programs from which many college students benefit. Yet, there is little federal investment directed toward success for non-college-bound youth.

The primary federal job training program for the "forgotten half" is Title II of the Job Training Partnership Act (JTPA). Only poor people are eligible for services under the JTPA program, and JTPA is so under-funded that only 5% of the eligible poor receive services. To make matters worse, in the past there have been abuses of the JTPA program, and provided services were often of poor quality. The Congress recently passed amendments that we hope will address abuses in the program. Still, since JTPA is woefully under-funded and targeted at only the poor, it barely makes a dent in the need. The JTPA and other targeted programs must remain a part of the mix of available programs, but we must do much more.

We have seen a dramatic decline in earnings for those who do not graduate from college, in part because of structural changes that have moved us from a manufacturing to a service-based economy, increasing global competition, and our failure to help the forgotten half. The *Washington Post* reported that the difference in earnings between high school graduates and workers with just one to three years of training is $5,263 in annual pay, or 19% for men and 21% for women.

As the National Center on Education and the Economy illustrated in the report, *America's Choice: High Skills or Low Wages*:

> The choice that America faces is a choice between high skills and low wages. Gradually, silently, we are choosing low wages. We still have time to make the other choice — one that will lead us to make the other choice — one that will lead us to a more prosperous future. But to make this choice we must fundamentally change our approach to work and education.[6]

The United States is the only industrialized nation in the world that lacks a comprehensive school-to-work system. The *America's Choice* report suggested that one way for this nation to begin to move toward a more prosperous future is to create such a system. The School-to-Work Opportunities Act is a valuable step toward this goal. The School-to-Work Opportunities Act is about giving people opportunities to succeed. It's about investing in human capital and giving people hope.

School-to-work programs are not higher education as we traditionally use that term; they are "hire" education — they prepare people for work. On 4 May 1994, President Clinton signed the School-to-Work Opportunities Act into law. I am proud of this accomplishment.

Youth Training Hearings

My involvement in the development of the School-to-Work Opportunities Act began with set of hearings I held as chairman of the Senate subcommittee with jurisdiction over job training programs. In December 1992, the Subcommittee on Employment and Productivity held two hearings to examine the successes of existing youth training programs and to explore the areas where changes were needed.

At the hearings, much of the testimony focused on ways to improve our current system of providing training to young people in need. Several witnesses pointed out the need for more business involvement. Businesses know what skills are needed in the workforce. Their participation is crucial to making sure we educate young people to be prepared for work. In addition, several witnesses testified about our methods of education. Traditional book learning does not work for all students.

In fact, most people learn better by doing and then connecting that to traditional lessons. Applied-skills training can be very effective. Many students need to see the practical application of what they are learning. We have all heard students ask, "Why do I need to learn this? I'm never going to use this in real life." Some of us have even been the ones voicing those complaints. Applied-skills training responds to that complaint by showing young people the practical applications of learning. Applied-skills training can be even more effective when some of the training takes place at the workplace, where students can see how learning is important to developing a career.

Much of the testimony was useful as we evaluated our education system, but one of the most compelling testimonies came from a young man who had turned his life around through a Boston program called Youth Build. John James is a young man from a troubled area of inner-city Boston. He testified that he was a high school dropout, a former gang member, and a former drug dealer. He said, "My family looked at me as a worthless kid. They didn't respect me at all."[7] Youth Build gave him a chance to succeed. Through the program he earned a GED and became an apprentice carpenter with a successful career ahead of him. Now he is a role model in his neighborhood. I asked John how many of the members of his gang would enter a program like Youth Build if they were given an opportunity. He said that at least 15 of the 20 gang members would jump at the opportunity. John's powerful testimony clearly illustrates the importance of giving people a chance.

Through the hearings and additional study, I determined that we needed to do more at the federal level to encourage the development of work-based training programs. President Clinton had demonstrated strong support for these programs throughout the presidential campaign, and he had been a leader in developing such programs in Arkansas. In his campaign book, *Putting People First*, the President expressed his desire to:

> Bring business, labor, and education leaders together to develop a national apprenticeship-style program that offers non-college-bound students valuable skills training, with the promise of good jobs when they graduate.[8]

In his state of the union address, the President reiterated this commitment, pledging a significant expansion of youth apprenticeship-style programs. In addition, Richard Riley, the new Secretary of Education, and Robert Reich, the new Secretary of Labor, both emphasized the importance of investing in human capital. I believed that the time had come to move aggressively on this issue.

Career Pathways

Soon after the inauguration, my staff began working with Senator Harris Wofford's office to put together a legislative proposal to encourage the development of a national school-to-work system. Senator Wofford is an old friend whom I first met when I was a very young, green, state legislator in Illinois. Martin Luther King had asked me to speak at the first anniversary of the bus boycott down in Montgomery, Alabama. When I got to Montgomery, I befriended an eager young man named Harris Wofford; and our paths have crossed many times since, most recently when he was appointed, and later elected, to serve as the junior senator from Pennsylvania. In fact, Senator Wofford and I joked that we had our own "youth apprenticeship" in the days we first met during the civil rights struggles.

Before coming to the Senate, Senator Wofford headed the Department of Labor and Industry in Pennsylvania and learned a great deal about youth apprenticeships as he developed the Pennsylvania Youth Apprenticeship program. Pennsylvania is a model state in moving progressively on the school-to-work transition issue, and much of the credit is due to Harris Wofford's effective leadership. Senator Wofford's expertise proved invaluable as we worked to fashion our proposal.

On 25 February 1993, Senator Wofford and I introduced the Career Pathways Act of 1993. In drafting our legislation, Senator Wofford and I drew from my hearings on youth training, as well as from a wealth of proposals and suggestions from educators, labor, industry, and youth program representatives. We particularly relied on the work of Sam Halperin, Trish McNeil, Alan Zuckerman, and others with the American Youth Policy Forum, as well as Hilary Pennington from Jobs for the Future. Other members of Congress, including Senator Kennedy, Senator Nunn, Senator Breaux, Representative Goodling, and Representative Gunderson, had worked actively on this issue; we also drew from their work.

Through our study we determined that we should recognize some key principles to guide us in formulating our bill:

1. The use of the term *youth apprenticeship* is misleading. These programs are not apprenticeship programs as they traditionally have been known in this country. They have some similar elements. But they do not track participants into a narrow career choice, and they do not come with the guarantee of a job. Some programs are more like pre-apprenticeships; others are like career academies; others are a little different from either. Many people have struggled with what to call these programs: "apprenticeship-like," "apprenticeship-style," "pre-apprenticeship," "work-based learning"? We chose to call them "career pathways," which exemplifies the goals of this concept — to create career pathways or options for *all* young people.

2. The best way to establish a national school-to-work system is from the ground up, building on local and state successes.

3. There is not one specific model for a successful school-to-work program. As long as certain basic elements are there, local people must be given the flexibility to fashion programs that meet their needs.

4. Employers should get involved because this is a part of their necessary human capital investments. However, while some incentives may be necessary — particularly for small employers — we shouldn't provide any financial incentives until we can better evaluate what those should be.

5. European models have illustrated that there should be a greater role for industry and trade associations in the development of

136

national standards and occupation-specific school-to-work transition. There is a role for the federal government to help support that.

6. A successful, national school-to-work transition system should not be targeted at a specific income group or the "forgotten half." A successful national system will create options for all youth; otherwise the system will be seen as just another "track" for non-college-bound youth.

We also determined what we believed were the basic elements for successful work-based training programs:

- an integration of school-based learning with worksite learning;
- training and orientation for teachers and worksite mentors and supervisors;
- high academic standards that maintain future career options;
- occupational and technical training;
- instruction in employability skills (work-readiness skills);
- work-based learning (structured training at the worksite);
- pre-enrollment career counseling and academic support;
- career guidance and academic support throughout the program;
- skill certification or postsecondary education credit for all graduates;
- active collaboration among all involved in program design, implementation, and ongoing innovation;
- methods to assess academic mastery, work-related skills, and preparedness for postsecondary work or educational programs;
- assurances that federal and state worker-protection laws apply to students;
- program admission criteria that are consistent with all federal civil rights laws;
- training options and career counseling that address nontraditional employment for women and that facilitate the entry of minorities and women into high-skill, high-wage professions; and
- systematic efforts to place graduates in post-program employment or higher education options.

Senator Wofford and I viewed the Career Pathways program as only one piece of the puzzle to provide a quality system for facilitating the transition from school to employment. We believed it represented a valuable step forward in providing a quality work-based program for young people in high school, but more needed to be done for those who had dropped out of school. In addition, the Career Pathways program was intended to work hand in hand with efforts to establish educational and occupational goals and standards, as well as systemic school reform, including the President's education reform initiative, Goals 2000.

Working with the Clinton Administration

After introducing the Career Pathways Act of 1993, Senator Wofford and I began working with the Clinton Administration to assist them in crafting a legislative proposal. The Administration was enthusiastic about school-to-work programs and considered enacting one a major legislative priority. Both Secretary Reich and Secretary Riley were committed to moving forward quickly on the issue. The Administration conducted an active outreach program in which they sought the input of everyone with a stake in the system. The stakeholders included the business community, organized labor, education groups, the job training community, and state and local governments. In the meantime, progress was made in Congress.

On 3 March 1993 the Subcommittee on Employment and Productivity held a hearing on the Career Pathways Act. At the hearing, several witnesses discussed the matter of which federal department should administer the program. The Career Pathways Act provided for administration by the Secretary of Labor in consultation with the Secretary of Education. While there was no unanimity of opinion, some witnesses expressed the view that the Secretary of Education should play the lead role.[9]

Another issue that received considerable attention at the hearing was the question of what the program should be named. Several witnesses agreed that "youth-apprenticeship" was misleading and were pleased that this matter was addressed in the legislation. In particular, these witnesses expressed the concern that the term "youth apprenticeship" could be confusing because there is a well-established apprenticeship system in this country. Using the term "youth apprenticeship" might create the impression that these youth programs complied with the same rigorous requirements of formal adult apprenticeship programs. Such an impression, they argued, could dilute the significance of formal apprenticeships. Representatives of organized labor were particularly concerned about this issue. I shared these concerns, and that is one reason we chose Career Pathways as the name for our legislation.

On 24 March 1993 Congressman Gunderson, Congressman Goodling, and six other members of the House of Representatives introduced the National School-to-Work Transition and Youth Apprenticeship Act of 1993. Representatives Gunderson and Goodling are both Republicans on the House Education and Labor Committee. Congressman Goodling is the ranking minority member of the committee, and Congressman Gunderson is widely respected for his expertise on training issues. The fact that these important Republican members of the committee introduced a bill promoting the development of a national school-to-work system was encouraging. It was clear that a bipartisan effort was gaining momentum.

Additionally, the Gunderson-Goodling bill contained an interesting proposal to address the issue of which department should administer the program. Under their bill, the program would be administered by an interagency compact established through the agreement of the Secretaries of Labor, Education, and Commerce.

The Administration continued its outreach effort for some months, giving all interested parties the opportunity to contribute to the process. A tribute to this effort is that the resulting School-to-Work Opportunities Act of 1993 was supported by an impressive list of organizations, some of which often come down on different sides of workplace issues. These organizations include the Business Roundtable, the Chamber of Commerce, the National Association of Manufacturers, the National Alliance of Business, the AFL-CIO, the National Education Association, the American Federation of Teachers, the Council of Chief State School Officers, and the National Governors' Association.

The School-to-Work Opportunities Act

On 5 August 1993, I introduced the Clinton Administration's School-to-Work Opportunities Act. I was proud to be joined by an impressive bipartisan list of co-sponsors: Senator Kennedy, Senator Durenburger, Senator Wofford, Senator Pell, Senator Metzenbaum, Senator Dodd, Senator Hatfield, Senator Moseley-Braun, Senator Breaux, and Senator Murray. On the same day, the bill also was introduced in the House of Representatives by Congressman Ford, chairman of the House Education and Labor Committee and a strong leader on education and training issues.

The School-to-Work Opportunities Act promotes the establishment of a national school-to-work system from the ground up. The act allows states to build on such successful programs as tech prep, career academies, cooperative learning, and youth apprenticeships and encourages the states to bring these programs together into a coordinated system. Secretary Riley and Secretary Reich outlined the primary features of the legislation in their joint testimony before the Subcommittee on Employment and Productivity:

> The proposed legislation provides "venture capital" for States and communities to underwrite the initial costs of planning and establishing a statewide School-to-Work Opportunities system. These systems would be driven by State and local decision makers and ultimately be maintained with other Federal, State, local and private resources.
>
> Although the legislation provides for a significant degree of local flexibility and creativity so that programs can address local needs and respond to changes in the local labor market, there will be common elements in all programs. All School-to-Work Opportunities programs would contain three core components:
>
>> Work-based learning includes providing students with a planned program of job training in a broad range of tasks in an occupational area, as well as paid work experience and mentoring; school-based learning includes a coherent multi-year sequence of instruction in career majors — typically beginning in the eleventh grade and including one or two years of postsecondary education — tied to high academic and skill standards as proposed in the "Goals 2000: Educate America Act." School-based learning must also provide career exploration and counseling, and periodic evaluations to identify students' academic strengths and weaknesses. Connecting Activities would ensure coordination of the work and school-based learning components of a School-to-Work Opportunities program, such as providing technical assistance in designing work-based learning components, matching students with employers' work-based learning opportunities, and collecting information on what happens to students after they complete the program.
>
> Students completing a School-to-Work Opportunities program would earn a high school diploma, and often a certificate from a postsecondary institution. They would also get a portable industry-recognized credential certifying competency in an occupational area. Most importantly, these students would be ready to start a first job on a career track or pursue further education and training. Under this legislation, States will have multiple avenues to build school-to-work systems with Federal support — development

grants, implementation grants, and waivers. First, we expect every State that applies to get a development grant, which can be used both to produce a comprehensive plan and to begin the developmental work of constructing a system. Second, once a State has an approved plan, it can be considered for a five-year implementation grant. The school-to-work implementation funds will roll out in "waves" with leading-edge States awarded the first grants with the understanding that their efforts are, in part, to inform and improve subsequent efforts. This will enable the pace to pick up as we go along. We anticipate that with sufficient funds we will be able to begin supporting implementation in all States over the next four years. State plans and applications for implementation funds must address some fundamental issues to ensure a successful statewide school-to-work system. These include:

> Ensuring opportunities for all students to participate in School-to-Work Opportunities programs, including students who are disadvantaged students, students of diverse racial, ethnic, and cultural backgrounds, students with disabilities, students with limited English proficiency, low achieving and academically talented students, and former students who may have dropped out of school; ensuring opportunities for young women to participate in programs that lead to high-performance high-paying jobs including jobs in nontraditional employment; continuing the School-to-Work Opportunities program when funds under this proposal are no longer available; coordinating funds under the School-to-Work Opportunities program with funds from related Federal education and training programs (such as the Carl D. Perkins Vocational and Applied Technology Act, the Family Support Act, the Individuals with Disabilities Education Act and the Adult Education Act); stimulating and supporting school-to-work opportunities program throughout the State.

Implementation funds may be expended for activities undertaken to help a State implement its School-to-Work Opportunities system. The legislation provides that such activities may include, for example, recruiting and providing assistance to employers; conducting outreach activities to promote collaboration by key partners; providing training for teachers, employers, workplace mentors, counselors and others; providing labor market information to partnerships to help determine which higher skill occupations are in demand; designing or adapting work-based learning programs; and working with other States that are developing or implementing School-to-Work Opportunities systems. In addition, funds authorized by the legislation could be used, for example, to provide services to individuals who require additional support in order to participate effectively in School-to-Work Opportunities. Third, States will also have the opportunity to seek waivers to provisions of related Federal education and job training programs. Waivers are an additional resource to assist in the start up and implementation of School-to-Work Opportunities programs and to facilitate coordination between this new effort and existing programs. Though the pace of program expansion will depend on the amount of funds appropriated for the legislation, we have structured the initiative to enable rapid, nationwide activity. Fourth, the legislation also authorizes support for direct Federal grants to local communities that are prepared to implement a School-to-Work Opportunities program, but that are in States not yet ready for implementation. Fifth, grants will be available for urban and rural areas characterized by high unemployment and poverty, to give these areas special support to help overcome the substantial challenges they face in building effective School-to-Work Opportunities programs. Finally, funds are also provided to the Secretaries to offer training and technical assistance to States, local partnership and others, to conduct research and demonstration projects and, in collaboration with States, to establish performance standards.[10]

The Administration did a great job putting the legislation together; and the bill enjoyed strong bipartisan support in Congress, as well as the support of major business, labor, and education organizations. This helped immeasurably as we pushed the bill through the legislative process.

While the bill moved with relative ease through the Congress, its passage was not without some controversy. There were, of course, a number of concerns that we were able to address or fine-tune without much difficulty. For example, my colleague from Iowa, Senator Harkin, who chairs the Subcommittee on Disabilities, looked at some of the existing programs and found that they were less than ideal in terms of providing opportunities to students with disabilities. In the House, similar concerns were expressed regarding the accessibility of the programs to other at-risk populations, such as high school dropouts. We were able to address these issues through modifications worked out through the legislative process.

A few important issues reached the level of full-fledged controversy. They included the consolidation and coordination of existing job training programs, the type of work experience that was to be part of any school-to-work program, and the governance of the program in the states.

Issues

Consolidation/Coordination of Job Training Programs. During committee and floor consideration of the School-to-Work Opportunities Act, the question of whether there are "too many job training programs" and how the programs could be consolidated or coordinated were discussed at length. A report by the U.S. General Accounting Office (GAO) had attracted attention to the issue; and Senator Kassebaum, the ranking Republican on the Senate Labor and Human Resources Committee, frequently raised it as a concern.

Consolidation and coordination of job training programs are sorely needed. But during the debate the issue was greatly exaggerated, sometimes in a legitimate effort to make a policy argument, sometimes out of misunderstanding, and in the case of a few of my Republican colleagues not on the committee, in a blatant effort to stall the Clinton agenda.

The Government Accounting Office (GAO) sought to list every federal program with even a mention of job training as part of its purpose. The final report identified 154 programs administered by 14 agencies with a total cost of $25 billion. In requesting the GAO report, Senator Kennedy intended to lay the groundwork for a comprehensive effort to reform the delivery of education and training services. The report was useful in this effort because it helped to identify some of the issues that needed to be a addressed. But the "154 programs" quickly became headline material, a rallying cry both for those genuinely concerned about too many programs and for those looking to derail a popular, bipartisan education proposal from the new Democratic Administration.

Of course, the number 154 had little direct relevance to the coordination issue, because the GAO report was so broad in its scope. Large programs were split by GAO into their many components, adding to the count: the Carl Perkins Vocational and Technical Education Act counted as more than 20 programs; the Job Training Partnership Act (JTPA) counted as more than 20 programs; and each federal student grant and loan program counted as a separate program. Significantly, the student grant and loan programs account for nearly $9 billion of the $25 billion that GAO attributes to employment and training programs. In addition, GAO counts a number of programs that have never been funded, some that are funded at very low levels, and still others that are only tangentially related to training, such as Health Care for Homeless Veterans.

Even with these flaws, the GAO report served a valuable purpose by focusing more attention on this important issue. Several members requested follow-up studies to more clearly outline the issues. I asked the GAO to identify barriers to the coordination of programs (such as planning and funding cycles), common definitions, and governance structures. Senator Hatfield requested the GAO to identify problems in the administration of different programs, and Senator Kassebaum requested a review of outcome measures used to determine program success.

After introduction of the School-to-Work Opportunities Act, my staff began a series of negotiations with Senator Kassebaum's staff and the staffs of other committee Republicans. The Departments of Education and Labor were active participants in these negotiations. Numerous changes were made to the bill in order to accommodate Senator Kassebaum's concerns about consolidation, business participation, and other issues. We seemed to be making progress toward gaining Senator Kassebaum's support. Ultimately, however, Senator Kassebaum decided to oppose the School-to Work Opportunities Act, and her stated reason was the need for consolidation.

I have great respect for Senator Kassebaum, particularly on education issues; and I am sure her concerns on the consolidation issue are sincere. But her decision was both disappointing and confusing to those of us supporting the School-to-Work Opportunities Act. A central focus of the School-to-Work Opportunities Act is an effort to address the issue of coordinated services in a responsible way, by encouraging states to coordinate such existing youth training programs as vocational education, youth apprenticeship, coop education, tech prep, and other programs into a school-to-work system. More than in any other education or training program, the bill provides the Secretaries of Education and Labor with the authority to waive provisions of law or regulations that hinder coordination. The Secretaries are granted broad authority and, in fact, are encouraged to grant such waivers. Senator Kassebaum did not propose any additional or alternative language to address the coordination and consolidation issue.

Furthermore, the School-to-Work Opportunities Act does not create a new, categorical program that continues to provide a separate stream of funding. It is a temporary program that provides seed money to states to encourage them to establish comprehensive systems. Each state will receive one five-year grant to establish such a system. After five years, the federal seed money goes away, and the states must operate the system with other funds. In fact, in order to receive a grant in the first place, the state must identify how they will fund the system after the federal grant runs out.

Given that the School-to-Work Opportunities Act represents one of the first major efforts to encourage better coordination of youth-training programs, it is ironic that program coordination became the primary argument used by opponents of the bill. And it is regrettable that Senator Kassebaum's opposition, which I am certain was sincere, provided cover for a few partisan Republicans who wanted to oppose any initiative of the Clinton Administration.

No single political party can be blamed for the proliferation of job training programs, and no single political party can take credit for the modest progress that has been made so far to address the issue. In fact, I worked with the Bush Administration on amendments to the JTPA program that authorize states to consolidate several existing, separate vocational education and training councils into a single Human Resources Investment Council, giving them the ability to cut across programs and develop a comprehensive workforce training strategy. In the current Administration, in addition to the strong coordination language in the school-to-work program, the recently proposed Re-employment Act would consolidate separate programs for dislocated workers into one comprehensive system for retraining and includes a proposal for One-Stop Career Centers that will go a long way toward making the entire system more accessible to those in need of assistance. The President also has established a commission to study coordination and consolidation, particularly in the context of welfare reform and changes proposed in the dislocated-worker programs. These initiatives build on the JTPA reforms and other efforts, including legislation that I authored to pilot program consolidation in some Native American education and training programs.

Paid Work Experience. As originally introduced, the bill required each school-to-work program to provide students with paid work experience. Some claimed that this requirement would discourage the participation of small businesses, saying that it amounted to another government mandate on business. Senator Thurmond, the ranking Republican on my subcommittee, was particularly concerned about this issue.

I had difficulty understanding the argument that this was a mandate on business. In the first place, the bill did not mandate any business to participate — it was purely voluntary. Second, the bill did not require every participating business to provide work experience — it only required that the *overall* program include some paid work experience. Moreover, the bill did not even require that the program's paid work component be for any significant duration. Interpreting the language of the bill literally, the paid work experience language could have been satisfied by one student being paid for one hour of work. This hardly seemed to be an onerous requirement.

To be fair, the rhetoric of supporters of the bill did suggest that paid work experience should be provided to all participating students. While the bill never actually contained such a requirement, many (myself included) emphasized the importance of paid work experience in work-based training programs.

In the Senate, we resolved this issue by changing the requirement that programs include paid work experience to a requirement that programs include work experience, remaining silent on whether the students are paid. We also included language to encourage programs to provide paid work experience where practical. With this compromise we were able to gain the support of Senator Thurmond and several other Republican senators.

The House-passed version of the bill contained the original language on paid work. The dynamic was different on the House side, where the House Republicans were strong advocates of paid work. In conference we resolved the issue by requiring that the program contain only work experience, but priority for funding would be given to programs that emphasized paid work.

Governance. In order for a state to receive a planning or implementation grant, the School-to-Work Opportunities Act required the state to submit an application. As originally introduced, the bill did not specify the entity within the state responsible for submitting the application. The bill merely said that the "state" would apply and submit a plan. This ambiguity resulted in a power struggle between the governors and the chief state school officers. This is a battle that is fought many times as we work on education issues at the federal level. The governor is the chief elected official in each state, but many states provide the chief state school officer with authority to exercise primary jurisdiction over education programs. In fact, in some states, this authority is granted in the state's constitution. The issue is further complicated by the fact that states choose their chief state school officer in a variety of different ways. In some states they are elected, in other states they are appointed by the governor, and in still others they are chosen by the state board of education. States also chose state boards in a variety of ways.

In Congress, we frequently wrestle with the governance issue on education legislation. Traditionally, the Senate leans toward the governors' point of view, the House toward the chiefs'. That may be because, like governors, senators represent whole states. Or perhaps it's because there are a number of former governors in the Senate. In any event, the School-to-Work Opportunities Act was no exception to this rule.

As we moved toward consideration of the bill in the Senate Labor and Human Resources Committee, Senator Durenberger's office advised my staff that he was concerned that the bill's language might permit chief state school officers to veto an application submitted by a governor on behalf of the state. Senator Durenberger, a moderate Republican from Minnesota, was an original co-sponsor of the School-to-Work Opportunities Act; and he had been involved and supportive throughout the process. Republican support for the bill was important to us, and we were committed to addressing Senator Durenberger's concerns. In my view, both the governor and the chief state school officer had to be involved in order for a state to put together a successful program.

When the bill was reported out of the Senate committee, it provided that the governor would submit the application. But in the application, the governor would be required to show the support of the chief state school officer and other relevant state officials. When the bill reached the floor of the Senate, we modified the language to make it clear that the chief state school officer would not have the ability to veto a governor's effort to submit an application. However, the Senate bill provided that the Secretaries would give priority to states that demonstrated the highest levels of collaboration and support.

The House bill reflected the concerns of several members who wanted to protect the jurisdiction of the chief state school officers. Representative Pat Williams from Montana was particularly concerned. Montana is a state where the chief state school officer is granted jurisdiction over education programs in the state's constitution. The House bill provided that each official approve those portions of the plan that were in their jurisdiction. The governors believed that "approval" amounted to veto power.

In conference, we worked out a compromise that allows governors to submit applications without the sign-off of the chief state school officer but protects the chief's role in the process by allowing the chief to submit comments along with the application. The compromise also provides that priority for funding goes to those states that demonstrate high levels of collaboration and support from all involved state officials.

The conference report on the School-to-Work Opportunities Act was filed on 19 April 1994. A day later, the House of Representatives passed the report by a vote of 339 to 79. The Senate then passed the report by unanimous consent. (When the Senate passed the original bill on 8 February 1994, the vote had been 62 to 31.) On 4 May 1994, President Clinton signed the bill into law and helped to create a system of "hire" education.

I have long believed that the great division in our society is not between rich and poor, black and white, or Anglo and Hispanic. It is between those who have hope and those who have given up. We have far too many people in our society who have given up. This new law provides all students with hope for a bright future.

Footnotes

1. Children's Defense Fund, *The State of American Children* (Washington, D.C., 1992), p. xiii.
2. Jonathan Kozol, *Savage Inequalities: Children in America's Schools* (New York: Crown, 1991).
3. Ibid., pp. 148-49.
4. The William T. Grant Foundation Commission on Work, Family and Citizenship, *The Forgotten Half: Pathways to Success for America's Youth and Young Families* (Washington, D.C., November 1988).
5. Lester Thurow, *The Zero-Sum Solution* (New York: Simon and Schuster, 1985).
6. The Commission on the Skills of the American Workforce, *America's Choice: High Skills or Low Wages!* (Washington, D.C.: National Center on Education and the Economy, June 1990), p. 5.
7. U.S. Senate Committee on Labor and Human Resources. Youth Training: Hearing Before the Subcommittee on Employment and Productivity (11 and 17 December 1992), p. 33.
8. William Clinton and Albert Gore, *Putting People First* (New York: Times Books, 1992), p. 87.
9. U.S. Senate Committee on Labor and Human Resources. The Career Pathways Act of 1993: Hearing Before the Subcommittee on Employment and Productivity (3 March 1993).
10. U.S. Senate Committee on Labor and Human Resources. The School-to-Work Opportunities Act of 1993: Hearing Before the Subcommittee on Employment and Productivity (28 September and 14 October 1993), pp. 11-13, 18-21.

Concerns About
School-to-Work

By Senator Nancy Landon Kassebaum

Nancy Landon Kassebaum of Kansas was elected to the United States Senate in 1978. Now serving her third term, she is the ranking Republican member of the Senate Committee on Labor and Human Resources. The Labor Committee has legislative jurisdiction over a broad range of domestic programs — including all programs administered by the Departments of Education and Labor, as well as a number of health and children's programs administered by the Department of Health and Human Services.

Senator Kassebaum also serves on the Committee on Foreign Relations, the Committee on Indian Affairs, and the Joint Committee on the Organization of Congress. She has a B.A. in political science from the University of Kansas and an M.A. in diplomatic history from the University of Michigan and is the mother of four children.

The Senate Committee on Labor and Human Resources has jurisdiction over a broad range of domestic programs, including education and job training. In recent years, I have become increasingly concerned about the proliferation of individual programs that provide the same or similar services to the same groups of people.

In the past, the tendency in Congress has been to attempt to solve each new problem with a new program. Rarely do any programs, once created, ever disappear. As a consequence, we are left with a plethora of similar programs — each with a slightly different twist — which leaves their intended beneficiaries confused about which one they should apply to for assistance.

One of the first priorities that I established on assuming the ranking Republican position on the committee in January 1993 was finding ways to bring about greater consolidation of existing programs. This task seems all the more pressing, given the tight budgetary situation now facing Congress.

I identified job training as being in greatest need of consolidation. Some initial work revealed that what began as a few, limited programs in the 1960s has multiplied into a daunting array of more than 150 separate job training programs costing nearly $25 billion per year.

My position in opposition to the Administration's school-to-work initiative is best understood against the backdrop of my broader interest in comprehensive job training reform. Although I had little argument with the stated objectives of this legislation, I thought it offered the wrong answer to the right questions.

Impetus Behind Legislation

Several recent studies have drawn attention to the difficulties that young Americans with a high school education or less face in making the transition from school to the workplace. Of the estimated three-quarters of young Americans who do not go on to college, many find work. However, they usually end up in entry-level, low-wage jobs that do not require a high degree of academic or occupational skill. Many wander from job to job before finding stable employment.

Many possible factors contribute to this disturbing trend, including the continuing shift from manufacturing to service industries and increased competition from abroad. Congress has focused primarily on another possible cause: the shortcomings in young adults' knowledge, skills, and attitudes toward work. When surveyed, employers often respond that potential applicants lack basic skills in reading, writing, and mathematics that are necessary to succeed in the workplace.

A number of innovative approaches to addressing these problems currently are being tested. Among them are tech prep programs, which were first funded in 1990 through the Carl D. Perkins Vocational and Applied Technology Education Act. Typically, tech prep programs link the last two years of high school with two years of postsecondary education through a common core of courses in math and science, leading to an associate degree or certificate in a specific career field.

Youth apprenticeships and career academies represent other models of school-based, vocational education reform. These programs target youth in the last two years of high school and provide monitored, work-based experiences that are closely integrated with academic studies. Youth apprenticeships combine, at a minimum, the following basic elements: work experience (preferably paid), close integration of academic and occupational learning through a collaboration between schools and industry, and receipt of a high school diploma, skills certificate, or postsecondary degree.

While many of these initiatives have shown early positive results, they are still quite small in scope and are oriented exclusively to local labor market conditions. By contrast, many of our major international competitors have established comprehensive, formal national systems to prepare youth for entering the work force after high school. Concern about our competitive position has contributed to a broad and growing interest in creating a school-to-work transition system in the United States.

In May 1992, President George Bush proposed legislation to establish a national framework for implementing comprehensive youth apprenticeship programs. While Congress did not take any action that year, presidential candidate Bill Clinton outlined a similar strategy in his book, *Putting People First*, to "bring business, labor, and education leaders together to develop a national apprenticeship-style program that offers non-college-bound students valuable skills training, with the promise of good jobs when they graduate."

Congressional Action

A number of members of Congress also were interested in school-to-work transition legislation. Early in the 103rd Congress, Senator Simon and Senator Wofford introduced the Career Pathways Act of 1993. Offered as a first step toward meeting President Clinton's pledge to expand youth apprenticeship-style programs on a national scale, their legislation would establish a new grant program under the Job Training Partnership Act to help states develop and expand school-to-work systems and programs.

The Subcommittee on Employment and Productivity, which Senator Simon chairs, held a hearing on this legislation in March 1993. Hilary Pennington, president of Jobs for the Future, who has worked extensively at the state level to develop and implement school-to-work programs, testified about the desire to expand these programs on a national level. She noted:

> So we need to expand to reach scale. Some of that expansion could come from increasing the numbers of young people already in what have been called 'youth apprenticeship' programs, but that will not be enough. . . . There is a need for variety of career pathways; no one model will serve every student.

In the House, two Republican members of the House Committee on Education and Labor, Congressman Bill Goodling and Congressman Steve Gunderson, introduced the National School-to-Work Transition/Youth Apprenticeship Act. My colleagues' interest in school-to-work transition issues would later prove instrumental in garnering significant Republican support for passage of the Administration's proposal.

Preliminary Thinking on School-to-Work Initiative

Unlike the drafting of the national service legislation, where congressional Republicans were not involved, the Administration sought input from House and Senate Republican staff early in the process of crafting a school-to-work bill. Leslie Loble, special assistant to Secretary of Labor Robert Reich, and Ricky Takai, acting assistant secretary for vocational and adult education, were the chief liaisons to the Hill on the project.

On April 29, these two officials met with four of my committee staff members: Ted Verheggen and Carla Widener, who handle labor issues, and Lisa Ross and Wendy Cramer, who handle education issues. It is somewhat unusual that so many of my staff are involved on the same issue. However, because two federal departments were collaborating on the proposal, it was necessary to brief those on my staff who had responsibility for both labor and education issues.

During this initial briefing, Leslie Loble outlined the departments' preliminary thinking on the school-to-work initiative. A four-page concept paper identified six guiding principles, among them: 1) The initiative must be integrated with other education reform strategies and not create another separate program; 2) employers must have substantial ownership of and participation in the system; and 3) states and local communities must be given substantial flexibility and discretion in shaping school-to-work transition systems. Although I endorse these three principles, I ultimately concluded that the Administration's bill did not achieve them. This failure was an important factor in my determination not to support the bill.

Over the next three months, my staff explored a number of issues with both department officials and Democratic staff concerning the development of the final legislation. Although I was not directly involved in these discussions, I met regularly with my staff to see how things were progressing.

However, I found it difficult to get beyond my fundamental belief that creating yet another new job training program would be a mistake and that time would be better spent shaping a more rational system out of the efforts already on the books. At the same time, I recognized that the school-to-work legislation was an important priority for the President and that it had broad bipartisan support. It was clear that some version of the bill would eventually pass. Therefore, I concentrated my efforts on trying to keep the language of the bill flexible, the size of the bill small, and the cost of the program minimal.

From that perspective, I concentrated on how the bill proposed to integrate new school-to-work transition programs with existing vocational education programs, how much a new school-to-work program was going to cost, and what incentives the bill would provide to employers to encourage them to participate.

Introduction of the School-to-Work Opportunities Act

On 4 August 1993, the Secretaries of Education and Labor transmitted to Congress the School-to-Work Opportunities Act of 1993. The following day, Senators Simon, Kennedy, Durenberger, and others introduced S. 1361 in the Senate. Similar legislation, H.R. 2884, was introduced in the House. Senator Simon described the purpose of the bill as "creat[ing] a national framework within which States can develop effective systems for improving the transition from school-to-employment. It would provide seed money to States and communities to develop programs to integrate school-based and work-based learning."

The bill authorized federal funds to support the planning, development, and implementation of state and local school-to-work programs. Jointly administered by the Departments of Education and Labor, these programs would have three basic elements: work-based learning (providing students with paid work experiences), school-based learning (integrating academic and occupational skills learned in school), and connecting activities that coordinate the involvement of employers, schools, students, and parents in selecting appropriate on-the-job learning opportunities.

To encourage coordination with existing programs, the bill would allow states to apply for waivers from statutory and regulatory requirements for particular education and training programs.

Once the bill was introduced, the Administration, congressional sponsors, and business groups lobbied heavily for its swift passage. Secretary Reich had visited several youth apprenticeship programs across the country, and over the August congressional recess he came to Wichita, Kansas. Hoping to gain my support for the legislation, he suggested visiting a school-to-work transition program in my home state. Although it was not possible to visit a school-to-work transition program, we did tour an adult vocational training program called the 21st Street Project, a program run by the Cessna Aircraft Company. I thought this was an excellent example of the type of vocational education program — outside of the school-to-work models — that Kansas currently provides.

We also met with several local employers regarding a variety of issues, including school-to-work; but the Secretary left without getting my support for the bill. However, I assured him that I would continue to review the legislation and appreciated his willingness to try to work together on the issue.

Two more hearings were held before the Subcommittee on Employment and Productivity. On September 28, both Secretary Reich and Secretary Riley testified about the importance of the school-to-work initiative as a part of the Clinton Administration's overall workforce investment strategy. In a prepared joint statement, the Secretaries stressed their belief that the proposal "is not about establishing a new program that will compete with existing programs for limited resources . . . rather it is about putting in place the building blocks for a nationwide system."

The final Senate hearing on the School-to-Work Opportunities Act was held on October 14. Representatives of business, organized labor, state and local governments, and other interested groups testified largely in support of the bill. A number of areas of concern, including how to increase the number and quality of school-to-work experiences for women and students with disabilities, were discussed; and suggestions were made for improving the bill.

On October 21, I met once again with Secretary Reich and members of the business community: Harry Featherstone, representing the National Association of Manufacturers; Stan Maury, of the Business Roundtable; Bill Kolberg, of the National Alliance of Business; and Dick Lesher, of the United States Chamber of Commerce. I knew the business community supported the bill, and this meeting was held for the purpose of convincing me to support it. There are many times that I do agree with the business community, but in this case I found it impossible to support funding yet another job training program without making an effort to cut existing programs from the budget or to consolidate existing efforts.

Addressing Concerns with the Bill

Having seen the final legislation, I was disappointed that it did not, in my view, accomplish the goals the departments had outlined in their preliminary concept paper. I focused on three major areas of concern:

1. Proliferation of Job Training Programs. In 1991, Senator Kennedy, chairman of the Senate Committee on Labor and Human Resources, asked the General Accounting Office (GAO) to identify and analyze all federal employment and training programs. They responded with an astounding figure: 125 different federal programs with annual spending of $16.3 billion. The GAO subsequently revised their figures to include 154 different federal employment and training programs, administered by 14 federal agencies at a total cost of more than $25 billion per year.

One of my first initiatives after becoming the ranking Republican member of the committee in January 1993 was to follow up on Senator Kennedy's earlier request and ask the GAO to find out if these programs were working. While the results would not be published for another year, early analyses indicated that, while federal agencies closely monitored the expenditure of billions of dollars for employment and training, they did not collect information on participant outcomes, nor did they conduct studies of program effectiveness. As a result, federal agencies have little idea whether their programs are providing assistance or training that results in people getting jobs.

While many of the school-to-work transition models appeared to be promising, no comprehensive evaluations had been conducted regarding their long-term effectiveness. I seriously questioned the appropriateness of establishing another national job training program before knowing whether the investment would be worthwhile.

Many shared my concern about the duplication and overlap of programs in our job training system. I was told repeatedly that the bill did not create a new, categorical program but, rather, laid the groundwork for coordinating existing education and training programs for young people. I maintained, however, that several characteristics of the bill pointed otherwise. The bill had a separate authorization, a separate pool of funds, and a separate string of eligibility requirements.

It seemed to me that the answer was simple. We should take this opportunity to consolidate programs and eliminate duplication, not provide another mechanism for "coordinating" an endless stream of programs that are outdated or just don't work.

2. Paid Work Requirement. In my view, there were two major problems with the requirement that all students must have a paid work experience. One, it would prevent existing school-to-work transition programs that have no such requirement — for example, tech prep — from integrating into the school-to-work system. This would lead to more fragmentation of programs, not integration.

Second, and more important, I was concerned that the paid work requirement would limit the ability of businesses to participate in the program. The Kansas State Board of Education expressed these concerns in a letter to my office:

> The paid work component raises many questions for the western portion of our state where there is a large agricultural base, but industry is small. The lack of available work sites for students limits the possibilities and amount of career exploration that these students would have available.

Businesses can provide students with valuable workplace experiences in ways that do not require paid work, such as on-the-job internships for academic credit, school-sponsored enterprises, and job shadowing. Businesses that could not afford to pay students would be excluded from taking part in the school-to-work system.

Without the active participation of the business community, S. 1361 would be of little value in placing students into jobs. As originally drafted, businesses were given very little opportunity to have a role in fashioning a program. I pushed strongly for modifications to the legislation that would enhance business participation in all phases of planning, development, and implementation of the school-to-work system. This is one area in which I was successful.

3. State and Local Flexibility. School-to-work programs tend to be locally designed by educators and employers, often including elements from several different models. The legislation proposed to define broad guidelines and basic elements for school-to-work programs. However, as already indicated, at least one of these basic elements — the paid work requirement — would severely constrain the ability of local communities to design programs that made full use of their local resources.

To encourage coordination with existing programs, the bill allowed states to apply for waivers from statutory and regulatory requirements for particular education and training programs. These waivers were intended to facilitate the process of streamlining and integrating programs into a comprehensive system.

The Congressional Research Service, an arm of the Library of Congress, identified several problems with the waiver provisions as originally drafted, including how specific the legislation should be on what can and cannot be waived. I personally favored the broadest possible application of the waivers, to give states maximum flexibility to begin consolidating existing programs. I agreed wholeheartedly with the assessment of the National Governors' Association, expressed in a letter to President Clinton:

> New waiver authority is helpful to a certain extent, but as a nation, we will move very slowly toward the goal of integrated workforce development systems if each state must apply separately to each different federal department for permission to integrate programs.

While changes were made to the legislation to increase flexibility, I remained concerned that the elaborate set of waiver provisions actually would hamper integration of programs at the local level and prevent states and localities from structuring programs to meet the needs of local communities.

Countdown to Passage

In the weeks prior to the markup of S. 1361, staff of members of the Senate Committee on Labor and Human Resources met with officials from the Departments of Education and Labor and business groups to discuss their concerns and suggestions for improving the bill. The committee substitute offered by Senator Simon at the markup on November 3 incorporated several modifications that I proposed and that aimed at forcing states to identify overlapping programs and to move toward greater coordination. However, several of my concerns, including the paid work requirement, remained.

The substitute was approved in committee by a voice vote; I was the only senator present who objected. I noted my support for the concept but expressed my concern that, since the federal government already spends $25 billion on programs for job training, I did not want to see another school-to-work program piled on top of these ongoing efforts.

I was somewhat surprised at the strong reactions of my colleagues, who shared these concerns. Senator Durenberger agreed that "we do seem to have these programs falling all over each other." Senator Kennedy noted that later in the session there would be a proposal from the Administration to reorganize dislocated worker programs and indicated that he "hoped to focus on the area of job training" at that time.

Along with Senators Coats, Hatch, Thurmond, and Gregg, I submitted minority views to the committee report on the bill that was filed on November 10.

Serious efforts were then made by the Administration to get the bill passed by Congress before the end of the session on November 24. In a telephone conversation with Secretary Reich in early November, I indicated that, while I still did not support the bill, I recognized that there was broad bipartisan support — as well as support from the business community. Therefore, I assured the Secretary that I would not raise any objection to bringing the bill before the Senate.

The House of Representatives passed their version of the school-to-work bill (H.R. 2884) by voice vote under suspension of the rules on November 15. However, very little time remained in the session, and the Senate was debating two controversial pieces of legislation (the Brady Handgun Violence Protection Act and the crime bill). Therefore, it proved impossible to get the unanimous consent required to bring the bill to the Senate floor under a limited time agreement for debate.

S. 1361 on the Senate Floor

Less than two weeks into the second session of Congress, the Senate agreed to take up consideration of S. 1361 under a very limited amount of time for debate. The Goals 2000 education bill was then on the floor; and the majority leader, Senator Mitchell, announced that there would be only one day of debate on S. 1361. The Senate also agreed to limit the number of amendments to a total of 15.

Because of the limited amount of time for debate, I decided to let other members of the Senate know in advance of my opposition to the bill. I circulated a "Dear Colleague" letter to the other members of the Senate, outlining my primary objection to S. 1361, which was that it would "create yet another duplicative, stand-alone, job training program of questionable value."

At 10:00 a.m. on Monday, February 7, Senator Kennedy and I began our opening statements. I started by explaining that, while I was committed to helping young people make a successful transition from high school to the workplace, I did not believe this bill would accomplish that goal:

> Although the stated objective of this legislation is laudable and addresses a legitimate need, I will vote against the bill. My opposition is based on my conviction that it compounds rather than corrects the deficiencies of current federal job training efforts.
>
> Consider the fact that we *already* have 154 separate job training programs on the books. By passing this bill, we will have 155.

The federal government spends nearly $25 billion each year on these 154 job training programs, according to the General Accounting Office. Some of these efforts are clearly worthwhile. Overall, however, the present system simply does not work very well.

The School-to-Work Opportunities Act is a prime example of why our current federal job training efforts are so disjointed. Each time Congress identifies a specific group in need of training — in this case, high school students — it creates a new program, with new requirements and, of course, new funds.

We have to draw the line somewhere. We should not be debating whether we need more programs, but whether we need fewer.

The school-to-work bill claims to lay the groundwork for establishing a comprehensive system. I share the goal of creating a better integrated system to improve the transition from school to work. I do not share the view that this bill will accomplish that goal.

The place to start is with existing programs. Congress has already enacted programs aimed at the school-to-work transition. Tech prep, for example, was created for this very purpose. For years, vocational education — through programs like tech prep, youth apprenticeships, and career academies — has been at the forefront of preparing students for the working world.

I am pleased we are now refocusing our attention to this very important effort. But let's look at the right thing — and that is fixing a patchwork job training system in desperate need of reform.

Supporters of S. 1361 argue that this is not a new program. Yet, it has all the characteristics of one: a separate authorization, a separate pool of funds, and a separate string of eligibility requirements.

Immediately following my opening statement, I offered two amendments that I believed would advance the goal of the legislation to bring together existing programs into one comprehensive, statewide system and would make the school-to-work program more accountable.

Under the first amendment, states would have the option of integrating existing programs with federal funds provided under this legislation, without having to apply for separate waivers from each and every one of the separate rules and laws governing those programs. A letter from the National Governors' Association endorsing the amendment laid out the case:

> We believe this amendment would be a very important first step toward true integration of existing federal job training programs. . . . Currently, S. 1361 relies chiefly on new waiver authority to promote better integration of programs. We welcome this

new flexibility, however, we believe that it will not be enough. The federal government must . . . address the tough work of developing a coherent, integrated workforce development policy — or at least allow each state to put the pieces of a school-to-work system back together without a burdensome waiver process.

The amendment was accepted after I agreed to modify it to restrict consolidation of funds solely to the Job Training Partnership Act and the Carl Perkins Act, excluding the other education bills referenced in the bill.

The second amendment proposed simply to change the authorization from eight years to three years. While Senator Kennedy argued that an eight-year authorization was necessary to allow time to develop the program, I argued that, in fact, Congress would not be forced to review the success or failure of the program until the program was scheduled to end. Although we in Congress frequently suggest we will hold hearings and evaluate programs, rarely do we do so unless those programs are scheduled to be reauthorized. After a short debate, I agreed to modify my amendment to sunset the program after five years. That amendment was accepted.

In all, a total of 11 amendments were offered. One amendment was withdrawn; one amendment offered by Senator Slade Gorton that would allow the JTPA summer youth program to place participants in private-sector jobs was tabled; and the remaining amendments were accepted.

One of the most significant compromises was achieved by Senator Strom Thurmond regarding the paid work requirement. Senator Thurmond, a Republican member of the committee, had indicated that, while he would like to vote for the bill, he could not support the mandatory paid work requirement. His staff had conferred with officials from the Department of Education over the previous weekend, and it was agreed that the senator would offer an amendment to eliminate paid work as a mandatory component of all school-to-work programs. In its place, the bill would give priority to state plans that included programs that provided paid work experiences for students.

Final passage occurred on Tuesday, February 8. The legislation was adopted by a vote of 62 to 31. The Senate immediately requested a conference with the House and appointed conferees.

Conference

The House and Senate versions of the bill were similar but did have some notable differences. I had expected fierce opposition from House conferees to the Senate compromise regarding the paid work requirement, but in fact this was one of the first issues to be resolved with relatively little controversy. The House accepted the Senate position, eliminating the mandatory requirement and modifying the language slightly to reinforce their belief that paid work experience is still a critical element of a school-to-work program and should be given a high priority.

The House conferees also shared my desire to ensure that there would be effective congressional oversight of the new program. They agreed to accept my amendment that provided for a five-year authorization, but rejected language offered by Senator Don Nickles that would have set specific funding levels for each of the five years. Instead, the members of the conference committee provided an authorization level of $300 million for fiscal year 1995 and "such sums as may be necessary" for fiscal years 1996-99.

Supporters of the bill were divided over how to resolve the issue of governance. The House bill required the governor to approve those parts of the state implementation plan that were under the governor's jurisdiction, while other state officials would approve the parts of the plan under their jurisdictions. The Senate bill did not require this separate approval process. After a few weeks of intense negotiations, a compromise was reached that would allow the governor to submit the state's application together with comments from relevant individuals and entities. Those applications demonstrating the highest levels of concurrence among all interested groups would be given priority over other applications.

One of the final issues to be resolved was whether the House would accept my consolidation amendment. One week before the conferees were to meet to approve the report, my staff informed me that the amendment had been rejected. Knowing that I would lose if I requested a vote on my amendment at the conference, I nevertheless decided that I would raise the issue with my colleagues. Ultimately, it was not necessary to do so. Shortly before the scheduled conference meeting, my amendment was slightly modified and incorporated into the final conference report language. The conference report was then adopted by a voice vote.

On April 20, the House overwhelmingly approved the bill by a vote of 330 to 79. The next evening, the Senate passed the School-to-Work Opportunities Act of 1993 by voice vote.

President Clinton signed the bill into law on 4 May 1994, having postponed the original signing ceremony one week because of the funeral of former President Richard Nixon.

Where Do We Go from Here?

Prior to Congress completing action on the school-to-work legislation, the Departments of Education and Labor began awarding development grants to all states with funds appropriated under current national demonstration authority in JTPA and the Perkins Act. Implementation grants to a few states to establish these systems are expected to be awarded this summer (1995). If appropriations are sufficient, each state will receive one five-year implementation grant before the authorization for the program expires in 1999.

My guess is that funding for this new program will not increase significantly over time. Senator Robert Byrd, chairman of the Senate Committee on Appropriations, spoke against final passage of the bill. He outlined his objections in a floor statement, saying:

> Although I believe a program for school-to-work transition is one that is long overdue, I cast my vote against that measure to make a particular point. This Nation cannot afford to fund new programs while at the same time maintaining that existing programs cannot be cut.
>
> What concerns me greatly is that while we continue to create new programs, old programs just never seem to die. This cannot continue. We do not have the money to continue existing programs as well as pay for new ones. If we create new programs which better suit our needs, we should eliminate the old out-dated ones.

I am disappointed that Congress did not take the opportunity presented by this legislation to consolidate existing training programs for young people into one comprehensive system. However, we did take several small steps in this direction, including allowing states to apply for waivers from requirements of current federal education and training programs to leverage funds for school-to-work programs. I will be interested to see whether the waiver authority is useful.

There is growing bipartisan sentiment in Congress that the current job training system is badly in need of repair. I believe that we need to start over from scratch and overhaul completely the current system. In March, I introduced legislation with bipartisan support, the Job Training Consolidation Act of 1994, which takes two important steps toward achieving comprehensive reform:

1. The bill would allow states and localities maximum flexibility to begin immediately to consolidate the largest federal job training programs into a comprehensive system.

162

2. The bill establishes a national commission to make recommendations on consolidating *all* 154 existing federal job training programs. At the end of two years, the largest job training programs would sunset unless Congress acts on the recommendations of the commission or reinstates existing law.

I am hopeful that my colleagues in Congress and others who are interested in reforming our job training system will continue efforts to address the proliferation and duplication of programs in the existing system. Without a serious commitment for change, I fear that we will only continue to pump more federal dollars into job training programs of questionable value and effectiveness.

The Evolution of the School-to-Work Opportunities Act

By Hilary Pennington

Hilary Pennington is a co-founder of Jobs for the Future. She is nationally recognized as an expert on education and training issues and has worked with the federal government and states across the country to develop public policies that integrate economic development with human resource development.

Hilary Pennington holds a master's degree in public policy and management from the Yale School of Organization and Management, a diploma from Oxford University's Graduate School of Social Anthropology, and a bachelor's degree from Yale University.

The author wishes to thank Samuel Halperin of American Youth Policy Forum and Richard Kazis of Jobs for the Future for their comments and insights in the preparation of this essay.

On 4 May 1994, sitting at a high-tech desk built by students in a Michigan school-to-work program and surrounded by the blue T-shirts and smiling faces of students participating in similar programs around the country, President Clinton signed into law the School-to-Work Opportunities Act.

At a time of increasing partisan debate over such major issues as health care and welfare reform, the School-to-Work Opportunities Act was noteworthy for the broad bipartisan support it attracted, both in the House and the Senate. Its purpose is simple but ambitious: to foster establishment of a high-quality, universal *system* in the United States for helping young people make the transition from high school to careers and further learning.

This essay tells the story of the evolution of this act from the perspective of Jobs for the Future, a nonprofit intermediary organization that played an important role in helping to design the legislation. The essay has three parts. The first discusses the context for this legislation, how it came into being, and what is particularly innovative about it. The second describes the role that Jobs for the Future (JFF) played in helping to develop the act — using JFF as a test case for one of the ways in which the development of American social policy is distinctive and unlike that of our Japanese or European counterparts. The final section discusses the implementation challenges the bill faces if the vision it articulates for a successful system of school-to-work transition is to become reality.

The Context

For many years in this country, four-year college has been seen as the conventional route to careers and occupational advancement. Indeed, the premium in earnings paid to college graduates over their less-schooled counterparts has greatly expanded in the last two decades. However, only one-quarter of our young people attain a baccalaureate degree. One-quarter of any age cohort in the U.S. drops out of high school; another 25% completes high school but never begins postsecondary studies; and another 25% starts college but never earns a four-year degree. The United States has no structured, easily accessible system for helping this "neglected majority" of its young people to make the transition to careers, adult responsibility, and further education and training. And most education reform efforts over the past decade have done little to address this problem.

Over the past few years, several factors have combined to make the lack of a coherent system for helping young people make the transition from school to careers a major public policy concern:

1. The worsening labor market performance of high school graduates. Whereas it used to be possible in the U.S. to get a job at good wages with only a high school diploma, this is no longer the case. The numbers are telling: The unemployment rate among young Americans who seek work as soon as they graduate is about 25%; and that rate remains relatively constant (20% to 26%) up to five years after graduation, declining only slightly with more years in the labor force. There also is a growing gap in lifetime earnings between high school graduates and those with college degrees.

2. The seeming ineffectiveness of many of the last decade's education reform strategies to reduce dropout rates and improve academic performance. As Jack Jennings of the House Labor and Education Committee observes, the current interest in school-to-work legislation

166

grows in part out of its promise as an education reform strategy that can more directly address how students are motivated and how they learn. Building on recent research in cognitive psychology, the school-to-work "movement" emphasizes the power of learning by doing through hands-on, interdisciplinary approaches in the school room and learning in the community and the workplace. Like other current, systemic education reform efforts, the school components of these programs include more experiential instruction for all young people, new forms of "authentic" assessment, elimination of tracking, and creation of small, supportive learning environments within schools.

3. The impact of several major reports. The publication of several major reports (in particular, *The Forgotten Half: Pathways to Success for America's Youth and Young Families* and *America's Choice: High Skills or Low Wages!*) was enormously influential in defining the problem of school-to-work transition and framing the scope of possible solutions. The organizations issuing these reports, the W.T. Grant Commission and the National Center on Education and the Economy, followed their release with sophisticated communications and dissemination strategies, such as speakers' bureaus that delivered countless speeches around the country, conferences, working groups to frame legislation, coalitions with other Washington policy organizations, and so on. These publications and dissemination efforts played an important role in shaping the national policy discussion.

4. The increasing importance of a skilled workforce to the competitiveness of American business. The school-to-work movement gained further currency as a result of an American business perception in the late 1980s that business needed a different kind of workforce and skill-preparation system. Several factors came into play here. First was the growing recognition that preparation for work and preparation for further learning are not as different as they used to be. With specialized, high-quality, niche production requiring new forms of work organization, a number of influential business leaders began arguing that the mind/hand split of educated managers and unskilled or single-skilled laborers was no longer sufficient for effective productivity or worker security.

Second, many companies expressed frustration with school-business education-reform partnerships that seemed slow to produce results.

Third, shortages of skilled workers in critical occupations encouraged some industries (especially the metal-working, printing, and health industries) to participate in some of the early youth-apprenticeship experiments as a strategy for recruiting skilled workers.

167

Fourth, the growing presence in the United States of European firms or worker-owners trained in the European apprenticeship system — whether companies such as Siemens or Bosch, individuals such as Blouke Carus of the Illinois Manufacturers Association, or small firm owners in states such as Pennsylvania and Wisconsin — produced a critical mass of businesses convinced of the value of this kind of approach to their skill-preparation needs.

5. The popularity of European school-to-work systems among U.S. policy organizations and state policy makers. The impact of the highly successful European policies and systems for skill preparation was influential in the late 1980s, thanks in large part to the efforts of Anne Heald at the German Marshall Fund. The European training systems, which provide structured, non-university routes to a broad range of good careers, served as an example of systemic reform that inspired much of the American intellectual movement and early practice. In countries such as Denmark and Germany as many as 60% of young people enter careers through a rigorous multi-year program combining paid work and on-the-job training with related classroom instruction. Advocates of a school-to-work system in this country contrast the high unemployment, low status, lack of access to jobs in the primary labor market, and isolation from adult mentoring and responsibility of most American 16- to 19-year-olds with the high status, earning power, and significant amount of adult attention and responsibility received by young people in many European nations.

Taken together, these five factors resulted in the relatively rapid movement of the school-to-work issue from the sidelines to the forefront of policy debate and local experimentation. Participants in the budding school-to-work movement began to look beyond the walls of the schools to enlist communities in partnerships focused on improving the transition of young people from school to careers and further learning.

These school-to-work programs combined school-based learning and on-the-job instruction into a structured learning sequence designed to produce active, critical thinkers and engaged, employable future workers. The emerging school-to-work movement recognized that no single institution should be expected, as the schools often have been, to take sole responsibility for solving the problems of young people.

The combination of these factors influenced both how the School-to-Work Opportunities Act was developed and what its content came to be. It is an innovative and important piece of legislation, one that reflects significant evolution in the federal government's view of "vocational preparation" and in its vision of the federal role in and strategies for stimulating national, state, and local change.

The legislation's innovative features include the following:

1. It does not mandate a program model but leaves room for experimentation and local diversity. Rather than reinventing the wheel, the legislation encourages states and communities to build on the infrastructure already in place, such as cooperative education, tech prep, and other programs. Nevertheless, it does stress some basic, essential elements that every student participant will receive:

- A high-quality, on-the-job learning experience, requiring progressively higher mastery of occupational skills;
- An integrated curriculum of academic and occupational learning set to high-quality standards and built around career majors in the upper-division years of high school;
- A high school diploma enabling eventual attainment of a college degree; and
- An occupational skills certificate, recognized coast to coast, enabling entry into a first job on a defined career path.

Taken together, these goals offer a radically different vision of the upper-division years of high school than exists in most communities today. While the act does not prescribe how states and localities are to reach these goals, its clear intention is that funds available through the legislation are to be used to build toward this new vision, not to support incremental changes in the status quo.

2. It does not establish another categorical program. Rather, it uses federal funding as "venture capital," giving states and localities sizable five-year grants to build a school-to-work system. Funding will decline substantially over time; the federal goal is to promote ongoing community ownership of and responsibility for bettering young Americans' career prospects, not to create another top-down, permanent federal program.

3. It calls for implementation of the school-to-work system in "waves," starting with the states and communities that are furthest along in their readiness for reform and ending with the least-organized states and communities. Thus federal funds will go first to where they can make the most difference, and the federal government will be able to use leading-edge states and communities to generate and test new ideas and to shorten the learning curve for others that follow. Beyond initial planning and development money for each state, the bulk of the funds will be disbursed competitively, rather than according to formula, with careful, on-site visits by a panel of federal and non-federal reviewers (modeled on the successful process used by the National Science Foundation's Systemic Science Initiative).

4. It creates a systemic initiative, not just another program. To get federal funds, states and communities must demonstrate how they are pulling together related education and training programs and funds into an integrated system for helping youth make transitions from school to work. Specifically, the act encourages the use of other federal funds toward this goal, unlike much prior legislation that prohibits states from merging federal funding streams. The legislation's architects in the Departments of Labor and Education and in the Congress intend system integration encouraged under the act as a significant precursor to the upcoming reauthorizations of the Job Training Partnership Act and the Carl Perkins Vocational and Applied Technology Education Act.

Indeed, the initial $300 million authorized in the School-to-Work Opportunities Act is intended to leverage change in the way existing federal Chapter 1, Chapter 2, Carl Perkins, and Job Training Partnership Act funds (totaling $14 billion) are spent. In reality, the federal vision of the stakes — and the resources — is even higher: changing the way mainstream education spending at the state and local levels is structured in order to help all students make the transition to economic opportunity, whether they are bound immediately for college or not.

5. It epitomizes the "reinventing government" strategies of the Clinton Administration. The legislation was developed through unprecedented collaboration between the Departments of Labor and Education. A joint-staff team collaborated in the development of the Administration's bill; the funds have been allocated jointly and will be disbursed jointly by the two departments; and an office is being set up to administer the initiative that will be staffed by both departments. In addition, the legislation puts the federal government in the role of "venture capitalist" and system-builder, rather than regulator or monitor.

These elements are both the strength of the legislation and its potential weakness as implementation begins in earnest. On the one hand, the act outlines a radically different system for education and the transition from school to work, one that requires profound changes in the attitudes and behavior of schools, employers, higher education, and young people. On the other hand, it provides very limited resources, little guidance, few performance benchmarks, and no consequences for lack of progress.

Jobs for the Future's Role in the Development of the School-to-Work Opportunities Act

Jobs for the Future (JFF) is a national, nonprofit organization that conducts research, provides technical assistance, and proposes policy innovations on the interrelated issues of workforce development, economic development, and learning reform. Since its inception in 1983, JFF has been working around the country with states, communities, and employers to help them design and implement new strategies and institutions for economic and workforce development. Several lessons from our work in the 1980s convinced us of the importance of the school-to-work transition.

First, it was clear to us that if workforce skills were becoming increasingly central to economic competitiveness at a time when the number of new workforce entrants was declining, then states had to develop better ways of dealing with the places where people "fall off the track" of adequate skill preparation. The transition from school to work clearly was one of those places.

Second, most U.S. public policy on workforce development dealt with people only after they had fallen out of the system: dislocated workers, dropouts, etc. It was clear that policy efforts needed to move further up the queue — to structure transitions between jobs and between school and work so that individuals could achieve success.

Third, it was clear to us that many of the first-wave education reform strategies of the 1980s were making little impact on how young people are motivated and how they learn.

These convictions led JFF to focus its work increasingly on the needs of employed workers and young people still in school but performing below their potential. It also meant that we saw school-to-work transition, adult workforce development, and education reform as interconnected; this view accounts for the appeal of the European system to us. Thus in 1990 we embarked on the National Youth Apprenticeship Initiative, a multi-year program to research, design, test, and institutionalize a different model for preparing young people for careers and postsecondary learning.

Our subsequent involvement in the development of the School-to-Work Opportunities Act unfolded in three distinct phases: 1) work on early program models and proposed legislation prior to the Clinton Administration, 2) intensive involvement with the Clinton Administration and Congress in the development of the School-to-Work Opportunities Act itself, and 3) ongoing assistance in supporting successful implementation of the act.

171

Before discussing the details of JFF's involvement, it is worth reflecting on the general role we played as a nonprofit "intermediary," working across the boundaries of school and work and of local, state, and national change efforts. In this sense, JFF can be seen as a stand-in for many organizations that play similar roles in policy development in the United States, both on this issue and on others. In other words, the JFF example is interesting not so much for JFF itself, but for what it represents about the development of American public policy.

How did a small, nonprofit organization not even located in Washington, D.C., come to play the role we did? I attribute our success to a number of factors:

1. The issue itself cut across traditional definitions, turfs, and constituencies. School-to-work, by definition, crosses traditional boundaries and "issue turfs." Therefore, traditional interest groups that usually play a key role in shaping the evolution of major legislation did not focus on the act and its implications until the legislation's basic parameters were already in place and supported by a fairly strong consensus among its key proponents in the Administration and Congress.

Mainstream education reformers paid it little attention, as they were preoccupied with the challenges of the Goals 2000 act. The architects of Goals 2000 saw a connection between their objectives and those of school-to-work but did not focus on the evolution of the school-to-work legislation. Vocational educators were not in agreement about the implications of the legislation, and so did not mount a concerted effort either for or against the bill. Some saw the legislation as a thinly veiled threat to end vocational education, others as the wave of the future and a new lease for vocational preparation. Because of the legislation's focus on the "middle half" of American youth — those in school but at risk of sub-optimum performance — advocates for out-of-school youth and the second-chance systems did not organize around the needs of their constituents until relatively late in the bill's progress through the Congress.

Other interest groups outside the education community also did not perceive the proposed legislation as either a threat or an opportunity. Organized labor took early exception to the term "youth apprenticeship" and focused much of its effort on eliminating this concept as the rubric for school-to-work transition, fearing that casual use of "apprenticeship" might water down the value of registered apprenticeships for young adults. Labor also worked to ensure that any expansion of work-based learning opportunities for young people would not jeopardize the jobs of adult workers. But beyond these appropriate concerns, organized labor saw the value of this kind of skill training and commitment to young people.

Employers were relatively neutral. The bill contained neither significant incentives nor problematic regulatory mandates. Had the Clinton campaign proposal for a 1.5% training tax on employers been retained (something that many analysts felt would have been the surest way to develop a system in the U.S.), the story would have been different. As it was, employer groups, such as the National Alliance of Business, the U.S. Chamber of Commerce, and the National Association of Manufacturers, endorsed the legislation and saw a role for themselves in advancing the cause of a more skilled work force.

2. The President's personal interest in school-to-work made it a high priority. This personal commitment to youth was shared by key policy makers in the Administration. President Clinton's interest in the school-to-work transition was long-standing and passionate. As governor of Arkansas, he spearheaded the passage of some of the first state-level legislation on school-to-work. He was the keynote speaker at an influential conference in 1990 on the subject of youth apprenticeship. His campaign platform included frequent reference to his intention to build a "youth apprenticeship system" for the nation. Jobs for the Future helped influence some of the evolution of then-Governor Clinton's thinking. At his request, we had conducted a feasibility study for the Arkansas youth apprenticeship initiative and helped design the state's legislation and subsequent programs.

Importantly, the Bush Administration also supported efforts and twice introduced bills to improve the school-to-work transition. As candidates in the 1992 presidential campaign, both men reiterated the importance of this policy objective, which contributed to the gathering momentum.

Upon election, President Clinton appointed key policy leaders to his Administration, including the Secretaries of Labor and Education, who shared his commitment to this issue. Several of them, such as Under Secretaries Tom Glynn and Mike Smith, among others, had worked on the Carter Administration's significant precursor to this legislation, the unsuccessful Youth Act of 1979. They had the intellectual groundwork, relationships, and trust to move quickly on this issue, supported by outstanding policy staff (Leslie Loble, Ricky Takai, Trish McNeil, Carolyn Golding, and others) who worked well together. There also were a number of mid- to high-level civil servants in the Departments of Labor and Education who had shaped the federal activity during the Bush Administration and were enthusiastic supporters of moving it forward.

3. A number of promising programs already existed at the local level, thanks to independent funding from national foundations and some grants from the Bush Administration. JFF was closely associated with these programs, having helped spearhead the development of many of them with funding from major national foundations. We had developed some models and attracted significant media attention to them. We had documented these early attempts and their preliminary results for young people, employers, and schools. We had identified and developed leaders at the state and local levels who became credible sources of information, expertise, and advocacy as the federal legislation developed. And we had organized an informal consortium of states that supported common principles for the definition of school-to-work and became strong advocates for a better system.

4. Many of these model programs — and the work of JFF — went under a new rubric — "youth apprenticeship" — a "high end" vision of what a school-to-work system should look like, based to some extent on European models. In the end, these terms were abandoned in favor of the more inclusive concept of "school-to-work," but our early advocacy of youth apprenticeship was important. First, it established the notion of "something new and different" in response to a need for which the status quo was clearly insufficient. Second, it established a benchmark or standard for what a school-to-work transition system would look like in its most comprehensive sense. Finally, JFF successfully defined and gained broad acceptance for a core of "essential elements" of youth apprenticeship through its work with its National Advisory Group (an influential group of policy leaders from education, organized labor, the private sector, foundations, policy organizations, and government), its network of local sites, and its state consortium. These essential elements included:

- High-quality academic preparation through a more interdisciplinary, hands-on approach to learning that builds on recent research in cognitive psychology;
- Integration of school-based learning with work-based learning in which young people enter learning relationships with employers, master progressively more complex tasks under the tutelage of a skilled mentor, and take classes that use their work experience as a way of contextualizing and reinforcing the academic experience; and
- Structured linkages between secondary and postsecondary education to encourage young people to go on to further learning.

Minus the words "youth apprenticeship," these "essential elements" became the basis for the definition of school-to-work used in the Administration's draft bill. The definition changed only slightly as the bill became the School-to-Work Opportunities Act.

5. Through a series of grants from major national foundations, JFF was established as a central intermediary for school-to-work. We had the resources, independence, and credibility to undertake multi-dimensional work at the local, state, and national levels. JFF worked at these interrelated levels, using activities at each to inform and strengthen interventions at the others, because of our belief that changes at each level were necessary if the United States was to develop a more effective system for school-to-work transition, rather than a series of stand-alone programs.

Because JFF had experience working at all three levels, we were able to bring to both the Administration and the Congress much of what they needed in the early stages of policy development. We were able to connect federal policy makers to what was happening in the field, to emerging leaders at the state and local level who were not part of the standard Washington-based networks to whom the federal government traditionally turns for input. In turn, we were able to provide leaders from the field with an opportunity to influence the evolution of the national agenda, and many of them proved willing to spend significant time and resources to do so.

JFF does not represent any constituency or organized interest. We are not a membership organization. Thus, as nonpartisan "issue advocates," we were able to serve as relatively neutral brokers for the emerging school-to-work movement. We could bring different constituencies to the table and help keep them there; we were less threatening because we are not part of organized, and sometimes competing, interests.

As media interest in school-to-work grew (heightened in no small part by the President's highly visible commitment to it), JFF became an informal clearinghouse for media requests, helping the ten pioneering sites with which it worked, as well as key states in its consortium, to become the focus of significant media attention, which included major stories in the *New York Times,* the *Wall Street Journal,* and segments on the major television networks.

6. JFF and other organizations working in this field focused on strategies to create a better system for school-to-work transition, rather than an isolated series of programs; this focus helped lay the groundwork for some aspects of the legislation. From the beginning, JFF and other organizations working in this field have approached their work with the belief that the urgent need is to develop *systems* that improve educational and economic opportunities for all young people, rather than adding *programs* that make a temporary impact but fail to be institutionalized on a meaningful scale over time.

As a result of this combination of factors, JFF was in a good position to inform and influence the development of federal policy. The evolving strategies we employed follow.

Phase One: Pre-Clinton. Between 1990 and 1992, JFF worked on a number of fronts to test and establish new models for school-to-work transition. We were not alone. The U.S. Department of Labor initiated a series of local demonstrations and state system-development grants. The William T. Grant Commission, under the skilled leadership of Samuel Halperin, issued influential reports, convened meetings, and structured policy discussions. Dr. Stephen Hamilton published a significant book, *Apprenticeship for Adulthood*, which laid the intellectual groundwork for the field. Anne Heald at the German Marshall Fund sent many teams of Americans to Europe to look at the European systems and to use that learning to design a new system in "American style." The Council of Chief State School Officers made the school-to-work transition the focus of a sustained, three-year effort to raise the visibility of the issues and to channel foundation funding to several states to begin work on systems development. The National Governors' Association took leadership on the issue of skill standards and the importance of linking school-to-work with broader workforce development and education reform strategies. These efforts and others contributed to establishing an intellectual framework for school-to-work, a growing body of practice and research to inform that framework, and a group of advocates from diverse perspectives.

With foundation funding, JFF's National Youth Apprenticeship Initiative selected and worked with ten pioneering programs around the country that quickly became widely recognized models for what school-to-work was about. Together with Samuel Halperin and others, we hosted a December 1990 conference on "Youth Apprenticeship: American Style" in Washington, D.C., that attracted significant participation, including then-Governor Clinton and Senator Sam Nunn. In 1992, we won a contract with the Department of Labor to provide technical assistance to the "work-based learning" demonstrations they were funding. This contract allowed us to increase the numbers of programs with which we were involved to 25. We published a series of useful reports on various aspects of system design, costs, and policy issues; formed a state consortium and assisted in the development of legislation and programs in several states; and continued our advocacy efforts through countless speeches around the country.

We also worked with the staff of key members of Congress of both parties, who were drafting their own school-to-work legislation. By the spring of 1992, there were seven school-to-work bills before Congress, and more than 14 states had legislation in the works.

This stage of our work was largely foundation-funded. Indeed, as often occurs in American policy development, private philanthropy seeded the early intellectual and program activity on which a large-scale federal initiative later was based. With this foundation support, JFF was able to develop a "vision of the possible" through its local sites, concrete advice on policy and programmatic options based on real field experience, and a network of leaders and places that helped move the field forward.

The role that JFF played as an organization working outside the government and established special interest groups is a common, and distinctive, attribute of the development of American social policy. As de Tocqueville observed long ago, this country often relies on organizations and associations outside the government to initiate major social change. Non-governmental organizations, like JFF, that are expert at forming associations of stakeholders around common interests can be remarkably effective at influencing government action. In our case, the associations we formed and were able to use were as important to our impact as any content expertise inside JFF itself.

Phase Two: Development of the Legislation. JFF's efforts on school-to-work kicked into high gear with the election of Bill Clinton to the presidency. In recognition of our work on the issue and President Clinton's commitment to school-to-work, I was asked to speak at the nationally televised "Economic Summit" in Little Rock, Arkansas, held in December 1992. I also served on the transition team assigned to look at the federal structure for work-related education and training (examining both the U.S. Departments of Labor and Education) and then on an informal Administration task force.

In preparation for a meeting of our state consortium in February 1993, JFF developed mock legislation for state-level "youth apprenticeship" initiatives and a concept paper based on our experience at the state and local levels, recommending federal legislation and an implementation strategy. This early paper outlined the "essential elements" of school-to-work, proposing an implementation strategy through states and localities that would proceed via "waves" of competitive grants. It emphasized the importance of quality work-based learning and connections to postsecondary education. These ideas were adopted and then adapted by the Administration's key legislative design team.

In January, we worked with Samuel Halperin in his new role as Director of the American Youth Policy Forum to bring congressional and Administration staff out of Washington to look at model school-to-work and youth development programs. Legislative staff visited City-Year, YouthBuild, and ProTech in Boston. The American Youth Policy Forum continued taking key Washington policy makers to see exemplary school-to-work programs across the country throughout the next year.

In addition to efforts to get policy makers out of Washington, we also participated with others in attempts to bring the field to Washington and to build a coalition of Washington groups that could advocate for a common set of principles. For example, JFF brought state, local, and employer representatives to meet with the Administration's design team and congressional staff. With the American Youth Policy Forum, the Manpower Demonstration Research Corporation, and the National Alliance of Business, we co-sponsored a meeting on employer participation and incentives. Once the Secretaries of Labor and Education decided to launch school-to-work activity under their current budget authority, we worked with the National Center for Research in Vocational Education to design, organize, and facilitate a "bidders conference" for more than 600 representatives from all 50 states to orient them to the forthcoming development and implementation grants.

JFF testified before two congressional committees and organized a briefing for the staff of the Minority Caucus to discuss the impact of school-to-work programs on young people of color. This briefing emphasized the importance of structuring school-to-work as a comprehensive initiative, rather than a series of set-asides for special populations.

JFF also participated, with many other organizations, in several Washington-based coalitions that worked with remarkable collegiality to develop common positions on school-to-work. One was convened primarily by Samuel Halperin, another by the National Center on Education and the Economy as part of their broader effort to advance the agenda put forward in the *America's Choice* report. As a result of the work of these groups, many Washington-based organizations, such as the National Governors' Association, the Council of Chief State School Officers, the National Youth Employment Coalition, and others, already had endorsed a series of positions that were presented in white papers to the new Administration before it officially took office.

Phase Three: Assistance with Planning for Implementation. Once congressional debate began in earnest on the bill, JFF turned its attention to issues of implementation. Our lack of a physical presence in Washington and our predominant concern with the evolution of school-to-work initiatives in the field did not equip us to be major players as the bill actually made its way through the legislative process. Instead, JFF's work in this period had two major elements: 1) work for the Departments of Labor and Education under our pre-existing contract to provide technical assistance on the school-to-work issue, and 2) independent work through our foundation funding.

Under its federal contract, JFF was asked to address critical implementation challenges — preparing policy and strategy memos on issues such as two- and five-year performance outcomes and goals for the initiative, strategies for taking employer involvement to meaningful scale, strategies for increasing parental involvement, and so on. These were then used by interdepartmental work teams to develop the Administration's own goals and strategies for meeting them.

While staying a trusted source of expertise to the government, JFF worked to maintain its independence and to continue to advocate through its various networks for the kinds of things that would ensure more effective implementation of both the letter and the spirit of the new School-to-Work Opportunities Act. Together with our national advisory group, we developed a policy memo to the Secretaries of Labor and Education, outlining our concerns about aspects of the Act's implementation and suggesting strategies for handling them. We developed two practical documents for the burgeoning numbers of newcomers to the field of school-to-work: a tool kit for local practitioners and one for state policy makers. We conducted a series of trainings and conferences around the country. We provided technical assistance to states and localities. And we continued making speeches advocating for school-to-work and disseminating information.

Beyond Legislation: The Implementation Challenge

Today's school-to-work movement arrives as the latest in a long line of promising education reform initiatives. In it can be seen the philosophical underpinnings of John Dewey, the ghost of the 1970s career education efforts, and the integrating impulses of the 1990 Perkins Act amendments.

The history is not promising. As Richard Elmore notes, "It has been possible to do almost anything in American education, as long as one

179

didn't try to do it on a large scale, over a long period of time, or in a way that threatened the basic patterns of practice in most schools." Given this history, it would seem much more likely that this current wave of reform will result in better vocational preparation for some students than greatly transformed education for all. Designers of the current reforms have tried to avoid this result in several ways, including their emphasis on links to postsecondary education, the integration of high-quality vocational and academic preparation, and connecting "school-to-work" and "mainstream" education reform efforts to restructure high schools. Whether or not these strategies succeed remains to be seen.

Fundamental challenges face the field, such as attaining high quality rather than reinforcing the status quo under a new name, expanding to a scale that changes the learning experience for a large number of young people, changing established teaching and workplace practices, changing the nature of the high school experience, and creating significant impact from a relatively small amount of earmarked funding.

For the act to fulfill its promise and avoid the mistakes of past reform efforts, four crucial things are necessary. The current movement pays lip service to them but shows nowhere near the concerted focus and effort necessary if these are to become reality. First, school-to-work must ensure high-quality academic preparation, capturing the power of a more integrated, hands-on approach to learning and conceivably restructuring the upper-division high school years around broad, thematic, interdisciplinary "majors" in such fields as health, environmental sciences, manufacturing technology, and more. Research conducted by JFF and others shows that with these kinds of changes on the school side of the equation, student's academic performance (and their self-esteem) improves, dropout rates go down, and the numbers of young people going on to college rise. Without them, it is impossible for quality work-based learning alone to make up for long-standing deficits in academic preparation.

Second, the act must build structured linkages between secondary and postsecondary education to encourage all young people to pursue further learning. JFF's focus groups with parents across the country indicate that the most common fear about guiding a son or daughter into a school-to-work program is that it will deny that child the opportunity to go to college, which, in fact, is far from true. In programs that link secondary and postsecondary education, students enter a structured pathway not only from school to work but also to further learning at the postsecondary level. That will give them the advantage of earning while learning in a context that makes school more relevant and meaningful to them.

Third, the act must integrate school-based learning with quality work-based learning opportunities so that each reinforces the other — in other words, so that students are learning *through* work rather than being prepared in a narrow sense *for* work. To be most effective, school-to-work programs must not merely provide young people with "work experience" but must channel that experience into learning relationships with employers, so that students master progressively more complex tasks under the tutelage of skilled mentors and use their work experience as a way of putting their school experience into context. Ideally, young people in these programs also will earn certificates from participating employers, thus receiving a portable credential that employers throughout the country will recognize with higher pay and better job opportunities.

Fourth, the school-to-work movement must reach out early and aggressively to make employers and organized labor full partners. Much of the success of the European systems can be attributed to the ownership employers and workers take in the system and the responsibilities they bear for quality control, setting standards, and ensuring an adequate number of training places for young people. America has neither this tradition nor its related infrastructure on which to build. In many ways, this could be the Achilles' heel of our current efforts.

It will be critical to honestly assess the degree to which new initiatives address these issues. To use legitimate concerns about whether such changes can take hold as reasons not to try them risks shutting our young people off from hope for a better opportunity and denying the economy and American society the benefit of their talents.

Conclusion

Despite the daunting challenges of implementation, I believe the School-to-Work Opportunities Act represents a "change" whose time has come. The issue is not whether the country needs to build a better school-to-work transition system, but how it will go about it. This will require staying focused over the long term (and beyond the scope of this legislation) in the kind of ten- to fifteen-year effort that America typically has trouble sustaining. But we have no choice other than to try.

My hope for the legislation is that it helps the experience of the few early beneficiaries of these kinds of programs to become the norm for most young Americans — like those at Roosevelt High School in Portland, Oregon, which cut its freshman dropout rate in half as a result of its restructured career-majors approach to high school learning; like the American apprentices at the Lake Mary, Florida, Siemens plant, who scored the highest of any Siemens apprentices worldwide on their first year exams; and like Boston ProTech student Marsha Dennis, now on her way to college while continuing to work in her sponsoring hospital, who speaks best about the impact of her school-to-work experience:

> Getting an education means more than just going to school. . . .
> I don't take things for granted any more, because everything I do now will affect me in life later on. I know when to be serious. . . . If you had known me two years ago, you would have thought differently about me.

PART III
COMMENTARY

School Reform: The Making of Two New National Policies

By John F. Jennings

When Bill Clinton became President in 1993, he declared that he wanted to change the country and set about proposing scores of initiatives to revitalize education, job training, housing, transportation, the environment, and other areas of American life. But he also wanted to reduce the federal budget deficits that contribute to a growing national debt. Therefore, his comprehensive program for the country encompassed new spending for certain reforms within an overall limit on spending by the federal government.

Obviously, trying to achieve these two goals at the same time had to provoke great tension. Clinton wanted to reduce overall spending and then shift some of the remaining revenues to his new reform priorities. It would be hard enough to reduce spending, which would entail the elimination of certain activities that had been funded for years. But calling for the creation of new programs meant that the current ones would be under double pressure.

In 1993 Clinton achieved the enactment of a budget reduction agreement that is predicted to reduce the annual budget deficit by at least half. In the course of securing enactment of this law, he concurred in a congressional proposal for a five-year freeze on defense and foreign aid spending and on funding for many domestic programs. In regard to the other major domestic programs, he proposed a comprehensive health care reform that had as one of its chief goals trying to contain costs so that the effects of Medicare and Medicaid on the federal budget could be brought under control. These limits on health care spending would have been in addition to the budget freeze in the budget reduction law.

Although the health care bill, with its provisions to restrain medical expenditures, went down to defeat, the earlier enactment of the budget reduction legislation meant that Clinton and the Congress took some significant steps to rein in the federal budget deficit. At the same time, the President and the legislature also agreed on establishing many new domestic programs, such as a national community service program, the Goals 2000 school reform program, and the school-to-work program. Those are among the initiatives that Clinton believes will help to bring about necessary change in the country. Thus by the end of his second year in office, Clinton had secured success in both of his objectives: reducing overall spending and beginning new reform initiatives.

But the tension involved with trying to achieve these two goals permeated decision making in Washington during 1993 and 1994; and that tension is bound to continue through the remainder of Clinton's term in office, because he will be trying to shift more and more money into these new reform programs. That funding will have to come from previously created programs because of the budget freeze. In addition, there may be further attempts in the Congress to reduce overall federal spending, thus aggravating the budgetary tensions between current programs and the Clinton reforms.

It is important to understand the thrust of Clinton's larger agenda and to see its complexity. He is not merely asking for deficit reduction; he also is asking for additional spending on certain activities that will have to be secured by taking money away from other activities. This means that those who think that the growing national debt is the greatest danger to the country will not be happy with Clinton, because he is in favor of some spending increases. He is not enough of a "deficit hawk" for them. It also means that those who believe that the country's social problems are eroding the foundations of our democracy will not be pleased with him, because he is in favor of freezing federal spending and trying to reduce the deficit. Therefore, he is not enough of a "liberal spender" on social causes for them. And last, all those who are involved in any of the activities that have been eliminated or reduced because of the budget freeze and the shifts in funding to the new programs will continue to be unhappy with Clinton.

It is never easy to bring about change, but attempting to achieve such contrasting goals is daunting. Once we understand the Clinton agenda and the tense atmosphere it was bound to create, then we can more fully appreciate the circumstances in which both the Goals 2000 and the School-to-Work Opportunities Acts were conceived, proposed, fought over in Congress, and finally enacted.

In this concluding chapter I will discuss the significance of these two new national *policies,* the *politics* that surrounded their creation, and the *processes* that were used to bring them to a successful conclusion. All policies must be seen in light of the politics out of which they come, because policies are not abstractions. Rather, they are the concrete expressions of ideas as influenced by negotiations among groups. The final form of many policies are shaped by the processes that are used to get them enacted. Therefore, both the politics and the processes involved with the creation of new policies must be understood in order to appreciate their implications.

Policies. The importance of the new policies embodied in the Goals 2000 and the School-to-Work Acts have to be seen on several levels. First, and most significant, both reforms put the achievement of academic and occupational competence at the very center of schooling. Secretary Riley speaks in his paper about the need to raise the quality of the education being provided in American schools and about how the standards movement focuses on teaching and learning to bring about this improvement. Secretary Reich talks about the need to raise the job skills of American workers and about how an improvement in the quality of schooling is essential in that effort.

This focus on teaching and learning may seem basic, for what else are schools about? But many other reforms being undertaken today do not focus directly on educational achievement.

Those who propose vouchers for elementary and secondary education, for example, believe that market competition will ultimately make the schools do better in educating children. But that is an indirect end of a change in the governance structure of schooling. Parents, and not public school administrators, will decide where their children attend school. Similarly, many reforms that attempt to make schools friendlier places for children through better use of psychologists and nurses are aimed at eventually bringing about educational improvement, but that is not their initial focus. The same can be said about site-based management, more stringent requirements for teacher certification, and so forth.

By contrast, the Goals 2000 Act calls for a reform movement based on standards that will define what students ought to know and be able to do. The assumption is that the entire education system will be changed to center on these standards. Once a state has decided what children ought to attain, then the state's assessment system must be changed to measure those outcomes, the teacher training institutions have to modify their curricula to train new teachers in this subject matter, and textbooks must be changed to reflect the new material.

Integral to this standards-based, systemwide reform of public schooling is the idea that much greater flexibility can be given to teachers and administrators in conducting the operations of local schools once the academic and occupational outcomes are defined and assessment systems are put into place. Once those measures are accomplished, it is not so important to prescribe the conditions of schooling. If students really achieve a mastery of the subject matter, how they did it becomes secondary.

Jennifer O'Day describes how several states are now implementing systemwide reform, trying first to achieve this agreement on the results and then to give greater freedom to educators to choose the means of attaining them. Hilary Pennington shows that various states have chosen different paths to beginning school-to-work systems, all of which have the same objective.

This type of reform, which focuses on the educational and occupational ends and not the means, is very different from others being undertaken in many different locations; and it is especially significant in that it is supported at the national level like no other reform, as was explained in the introductory chapter. Therefore, it has to be understood if one is going to appreciate the influences that the national government is going to bring to bear on education in the next few years.

Although standards-based reform focuses specifically on content, the implementation of this change in our country's approach to education will have other effects, principally on the relative powers of the national and state governments as compared to local school boards. In the introduction to this book, I discussed how President Bush's advocacy of national standards for education was revolutionary because it proposed to shift to national groups the power to define what children ought to know and be able to do. This was a sharp break with our 200-year history of local control of education.

Fear that this shift would lead to federal control of education led to Goals 2000 being repeatedly amended during its passage through the Congress to emphasize limits on this new national influence over education and to declare a respect for local control. For example, it was made absolutely clear that the standards are meant to be voluntary; no state will be compelled to adopt any set of national standards. A state even can receive funding under Goals 2000 and have standards for education that are entirely different from the national standards.

However, the very fact that there will be national standards for education creates a pressure on state governments and local school districts to ensure that their students achieve this content. Parents will want to know if their children have learned the subject matter that the various national groups of teachers have agreed to as student mastery goals.

This leads to the second set of precautions that was enacted in Goals 2000 to guard against federal control of education. The national standards will be established not by the U.S. Secretary of Education but by national groups representing the nation's teachers in the various disciplines. To emphasize the limited role of the federal government in this endeavor, the law does not give the Secretary the authority to approve these standards. Instead, a new national council composed of education experts, state and local leaders, and business people will have the power to recommend the approval or disapproval of these standards. Furthermore, the power to approve the standards rests with the National Education Goals Panel, which is heavily dominated by the states — the governors and state legislators — even though there also is representation from the federal government, the Congress, and the Administration.

Thus the authority for the development and certification of the national standards for education is vested in these new national bodies that exist apart from the federal government and that are heavily influenced by the states and educators. The same type of restriction on federal control is manifested in the provisions of the law calling for the establishment of national job skill standards. The Secretary of Labor is not given the power to approve the skill standards that are suggested for the various industries and job sectors. Rather, the National Skill Standards Board, composed of industry, union, education, and other interests, is authorized to approve or reject standards that are proposed by groups representing sectors of the economy. As a result, there will be greater national influence over education and training, but it will not derive from the traditional pattern of aid and direction provided through federal departments and agencies.

Standards-based reform also will cause a significant shift in power at the state level. Currently, some states mandate a specific curriculum for elementary and secondary education, and a few more simply suggest a curriculum, according to the National Association of State Boards of Education. However, most states do not have a standard curriculum.

If a state accepts Goals 2000 funding, it must establish content standards for its schools. This will mean that many states, for the first time, will try to reach agreement on what ought to be taught in their schools. Then those states will use federal funds to begin to realign their education systems to reflect that content. As Gordon Ambach discusses in his essay, this trend to state content standards or frameworks has been under way for some years and will accelerate with the passage of the

Goals 2000 Act. For some states, the act will create a significant shift in control of education toward the state at the expense of the local school districts.

The last major policy shift signified by Goals 2000 and the School-to-Work Acts is a change in the federal role in education and training. As mentioned in the introduction, the 1960s established a role for the federal government in ensuring access to education and training programs for the disadvantaged, the disabled, and others who have special needs. But the debate has now shifted from questions of access to issues of quality. The various populations that have been the concern of the federal government now have access to education and training programs (although not fully for all types of training). The question is, How good are these programs?

The Goals legislation does not "set aside" funds for the disadvantaged or the disabled. Rather, it asks states to have the same high standards for all children, regardless of their condition. Neither does the School-to-Work Act emphasize the needs of special populations. Rather, it urges states to have a school-to-work transition system for all children. This is a significant shift in emphasis for the federal government. It does not mean that issues of equity are being shunted aside. Instead, it means that the federal government is recognizing that changes must be brought to the whole system if all students, including those with special needs, are to be served properly.

An example of the need for this change is seen in *The Final Report to Congress of the National Assessment of Vocational Education,* released in July 1994. That report showed that federal law has so emphasized the needs of the disadvantaged and the disabled that vocational education is in danger of becoming a separate track for those populations. A recommendation of this study is that the focus be shifted to improving the quality of vocational education. As a result, the beneficiaries will be the special populations, among others.

This shift in thinking was not made easily, as can be seen in Congressman Kildee's description of the problems that Secretary Riley had with the Democratic liberals on the House Committee on Education and Labor. And the battle will continue in the future in annual fights over the appropriations bills, because there is not enough money for all programs, either old or new. Thus, if funds are placed in the Goals 2000 and School-to-Work programs, then there will be less money available for the older federal education and training programs that focus on equity issues.

The main policy changes shown by these two laws can be summarized as follows:

- a greater emphasis in school reform on achieving academic and occupational content;
- a shift toward state and national influence over education; and
- a movement in the federal focus toward questions of quality in the education and training systems.

Time will be needed to see the extent to which these reforms will take hold.

Politics. The significant new policies at the national level heralded by the Goals 2000 and School-to-Work Acts can be better appreciated if we know the politics that surrounded their making. Presidents, cabinet secretaries, governors, representatives, and senators never have the political implications of what they do very far from their minds as they go about setting policy.

In the first book in this series, *The Past Is Prologue,* I solicited essays that discussed the introduction, consideration, and demise of President Bush's America 2000 proposal, the predecessor to Goals 2000. That program was the first to call for the establishment of national education standards and also for assessments to measure their attainment. The legislation would have authorized the funding of "lighthouse" schools, alternative certification of teachers, and a few other reforms.

The legislation died at the end of the congressional session in 1992 because a number of conservative Republicans would not allow the final agreement to be voted on in the Senate. These senators believed that the bill would lead to too much national control of education. The final bill had passed the House by voice vote, and there were probably enough votes to pass it in the Senate; but in the last days of a congressional session, a small minority of senators can thwart the will of the majority.

Although those few Republican senators actually killed the America 2000 legislation, support for the final agreement was not very deep among some of the other principal players. The Bush White House was lukewarm toward the final bill because the bill failed to authorize private school choice, and the President was going into a tough re-election campaign in which he needed the solid support of conservatives, Catholics, Christian fundamentalists, and others who favored that idea. Some Democrats in Congress also were not enthusiastic about the final bill because they questioned whether the bill was comprehensive enough to make a difference. A few Democrats also wondered if it made political sense to give a Republican President a positive-looking school reform bill that he would sign as he was campaigning for re-election.

It is clear that Bush's legislation, America 2000, was surrounded by a complex set of political considerations. Clinton's Goals 2000 also aroused strong political emotions, but the gridlock that arose from the combination of a Republican President and a Democratic Congress was gone. Therefore, a somewhat different set of factors affected the Clinton bill.

The Clinton Administration called Goals 2000 the framework for all the other education legislation that it intended to offer Congress. Secretary Riley, while governor of South Carolina, had fought hard to achieve enactment of a major school reform measure in that state, and he repeatedly asserted that the higher standards called for in that law had helped to raise achievement of all children in South Carolina, especially the most disadvantaged. The Undersecretary in the Department of Education was Marshall Smith, who for years had written about the need for systemic reform and who had served during the Bush Administration on the National Education Standards and Testing Council that had called for national standards and assessments. Michael Cohen, Riley's assistant for school reform, formerly was with the National Governors' Conference and had helped Governor Clinton and others to write the national education goals in 1990.

Riley and his bill drafters used the final agreement on the America 2000 bill as the starting point for their deliberations, believing that an agreement that almost made it through the last Congress would have little difficulty speeding through the new one. Unfortunately, they were wrong. As Congressman Kildee describes, the Democrats on the House Education and Labor Committee were willing to pass what they considered an improved version of America 2000 in 1992 because they had to respond to President Bush on school reform. But in 1993 they expected the new Democratic President to propose a much more comprehensive set of initiatives. Therefore, they were disappointed when it seemed that all he did was spruce up the last bill and re-submit it.

This dissatisfaction among House Democrats led to the hard time that Secretary Riley experienced in the House. He had to change his proposal to get it introduced; he had to accept further changes to get it out of committee; and then he had to work hard to get agreement on further modifications to secure a majority for the bill in the House.

All this came about because the House Democrats, especially the more liberal ones, wanted a big, costly education bill from Clinton — and they did not get one. This dissatisfaction provoked further questioning of the basic premises of standards-based reform. The liberals wanted to know what would happen to students who did not meet the new standards in poorer school districts. Would the states be required to intervene to help them? This debate took the form of arguments over the "opportunity to learn" standards and the Reed Amendment, which would dog the bill until its final acceptance in the Congress.

But after all the debate, the Democrats, including the most liberal ones, knew that politically they had to be with Clinton. And so they were willing to change their amendments to secure passage of the bill in the House, and they were willing to make further changes to reach a conference agreement with the Senate. Despite concerns about the equity implications of standards reform and about the limited amount of funds being provided, House Democrats realized that there could be no gridlock over policy as there had been with Bush.

The Democrats in the Senate were in a somewhat different position from the House Democrats. Senator Kennedy, chairman of the Labor and Human Resources Committee, was a leading supporter of the bill in the last Congress, and he continued to be a supporter when it was re-introduced under Clinton. Some Democratic liberals, such as Senators Paul Simon and Paul Wellstone, raised the same questions about equity that the House members raised; but they deferred to Senator Kennedy with the hope that in the conference the House would move the Senate bill in their direction, which did happen.

Because Senator Kennedy did not agree with the liberals on the equity issue, he found it easier to secure Republican support for the bill. He also weakened the Administration's original bill to remove the requirement that a state have content standards in order to receive funds, because he worried that such a requirement might not fit into Massachusetts' new school reform scheme. That action also served to move the Republicans behind the bill, because they also were concerned that it might be burdensome to some of the states. Therefore, except for the most conservative Republicans, the Goals 2000 bill moved through the Senate with broad bipartisan support. The problem on the Senate floor was the attachment of non-germane social amendments, "add-ons" such as school prayer and gun control provisions.

The House Republicans also included a very conservative faction that would not accept the bill; Congressman Boehner represents that point of view. These members believed that the bill would lead to too much national control of education and that other reforms, principally vouchers, were preferable to systemic reform. In the House, about one-fourth of the membership voted for this point of view; in the Senate, only about one-fifth of the members were in that camp, although 41 members did vote for an amendment to test the use of vouchers. However, vouchers were not included in either the House- or Senate-passed bills.

The Republican moderates in the House took a different stance from the more conservative members of the minority party. These members, led by Congressmen Bill Goodling and Steve Gunderson, criticized the bill as it progressed through the committee process whenever they felt that it strayed too much toward the liberal view that greater emphasis had to be put on equity. But in the end they voted for the amended bill when it passed the House, and they also voted for the conference report. About one-fourth of the Republicans in the House went with them on these votes. In the Senate, more than half of the Republicans voted for the final bill.

The Republican leadership in both the House and the Senate did not want Clinton to achieve any easy victories or, if possible, any victory at all. That meant that even if moderate Republicans wanted to go along with the Goals 2000 and School-to-Work bills, they frequently did so only after initial votes against the bills and after extracting changes in the bills, such as watering down the opportunity-to-learn standards and expanding the business representation on the National Skill Standards Board in the Goals bill. This was done so that they could claim some imprint on the legislation.

Republicans found Goals 2000 attractive because it was a successor to the America 2000 bill of George Bush, and School-to-Work was in the same stream as some legislation that Bush had proposed. Therefore, they would sometimes claim in hearings and markups that the ideas in the bills were really theirs. Of course, those assertions only increased the skittishness of the liberal Democrats who had their own concerns about the Goals bill.

Many Republicans especially liked the discussion of high standards, because they had asserted over the years that the Democrats were too concerned with issues of equity and had neglected the issue of quality. Republicans, as well as many Democrats, also liked the flexibility provisions, such as the waivers, in both bills. In a way, the Republicans were irked because Clinton and Riley had preempted them on these issues of quality and flexibility. The ideas were now Democratic ideas.

Among the national organizations, the National Governors' Association and three major business groups were the new players in national education policy making. Prior to 1990, the NGA and the national business community rarely got involved in any significant way in federal education legislation. But both of these groups were very influential in the consideration of the Goals 2000 legislation.

Since writing the national education goals with President Bush in 1989 and 1990, the governors had taken a much greater interest in the federal role in education. The governors also worked with President Bush and Lamar Alexander on the America 2000 legislation. In 1993 the National Governors' Association endorsed the concept of national content standards, which was very important because the development of such standards could have been seen as a threat to state influence over education.

When Clinton became President and former Governors Riley and Kunin became the Secretary and the Deputy Secretary of Education, they made clear that they intended to work closely with the governors — and they did. The Department of Education wrote its draft of the Goals 2000 bill in consultation with the National Governors' Association. When Riley got into trouble with the liberal Democrats in the House and had to modify the legislation, he continued to stay in close contact with the governors, including sharing with them the provisions of the bill that he was changing to mollify the liberals. The governors even got Clinton to weigh in on their side of the dispute by sending a letter implying a veto if the bill incorporated strong opportunity-to-learn standards and other provisions offensive to the governors.

In the end, the NGA was stymied by its own politics and did not endorse the conference report on the Goals 2000 Act. The chairmanship of the NGA and of its standing committees rotates between the two parties, and all positions endorsed by the NGA in effect must have the concurrence of both parties. Republican Governor Campbell, who was chairman of the NGA in late 1993 and early 1994, did not agree with the final bill, as he explains in his essay. And so he exercised his right to object to any endorsement, even though some Democratic governors wanted to support the bill. According to the *National Journal*, Secretary Riley was upset by Campbell's stand because Riley had tried hard to represent the governors' position.

The business community was more supportive of the bill. At first, they had the same concerns as the governors about the prescriptiveness of the opportunity-to-learn standards as proposed in the House; but they were satisfied with the compromises achieved in the Senate-House conference committee and so endorsed the final bill.

In 1990 the Business Coalition for Education Reform had been formed to coordinate the interests of the Business Roundtable, the National Alliance of Business, and the Committee for Economic Development. These organizations represent many of the biggest corporations in the country. The Business Roundtable, for example, includes the chief executive officers of the nation's 218 largest corporations. The primary concern of these three organizations was that standards had to be raised so that American children would achieve more in school. They had been through a period in which companies had supported individual schools or projects and had not seen an overall improvement in education. Therefore, they felt there had to be national standards for measuring state and local efforts to reform education. The support of the business community was important, because it countered conservative opposition to greater national influence over education through development of standards.

The national education organizations endorsed the concept of national content standards and supported the final bill. But during the consideration of the legislation in the House and the Senate, most of the groups were notable by their absence. Many of them shared the views of the House Democrats who were disappointed with Clinton because he had not submitted a large, costly program for education — or at least had not greatly expanded funding for the current programs. They also felt that Goals 2000, for the most part, was just a rehash of America 2000.

Two education organizations that enthusiastically supported the legislation were the American Federation of Teachers and the Council of Chief State School Officers. Gordon Ambach, the executive director of the CCSSO, gives his reasons for endorsing the bill in his essay. Ambach had served on Clinton's transition team for the Department of Education with Marshall Smith and Michael Cohen and had argued strongly during that crucial time between the election and the inauguration that the Administration ought to make the enactment of a revised America 2000 bill its first priority. Ambach also had served with Smith on the National Education Standards and Testing Council, which recommended in 1992 the development of national standards.

In addition to Ambach's personal views, the CCSSO had a strong interest in the Goals 2000 bill because it gave the state school superintendents both a role to play in school reform and some funds to distribute to emphasize that role. In many states, the governors and the legislatures had bypassed the education establishment by using independent commissions and study groups to give them ideas on school reform. The staffs of several state departments of education had been cut back because of budget problems in the recession of the early 1990s. Thus the Goals 2000 Act gave the state education leaders and their departments a much-needed boost in prestige and funding.

In the American Federation of Teachers, Al Shanker, its president, was a strong supporter of the idea of setting high national standards for academic content. He had long expressed his frustration at what he perceived to be mediocrity in American schools and believed that such standards would raise achievement. But Shanker broke ranks with his traditional allies among the House Democrats by opposing the stronger opportunity-to-learn standards that they had proposed, because he was afraid that those standards would shift attention back to inputs in education and away from demanding achievement outputs. Secretary Riley and his staff held Shanker's views in high regard and stayed in close contact with him during the consideration of the Goals bill in the Congress.

To summarize the politics on the Goals bill, the Democrats started out divided, with the Senate Democrats and the Administration together for the most part, and with the House Democrats mostly unhappy because of concerns about equity and the lack of resources. But the Democrats resolved their differences during the legislative process and were nearly unanimous in supporting the final bill.

The Republicans started out divided and remained divided. The most conservative members did not support the bill in the beginning and found no reason to change their views, despite the support shown by the national business community. Moderate Republicans generally liked the original bill and disliked the changes made by the House Democrats, but they swung behind the final bill after those changes had been modified.

The business community had the same views overall as did the moderate Republicans and wound up endorsing the bill. The governors remained divided, mostly for partisan reasons. And the national education organizations all endorsed the legislation with support ranging from avid to lukewarm.

Thus President Clinton achieved enactment of what he considered to be the most important bill he could propose in education. The final legislation was mostly along the lines of his original proposal, but there had been modifications for the liberals to highlight the opportunity-to-learn standards and for the conservatives to re-emphasize that all the standards were voluntary. It had been a difficult experience for all involved; but given the potential importance of the legislation, it was probably good that there had been such long and careful consideration of this new policy.

By comparison with the Goals 2000 bill, the politics of the School-to-Work Opportunities Act were simple. This bill received broad organizational and bipartisan support when it was introduced and retained that support as it went through the legislative process.

Once the Clinton Administration decided not to create a new, separate apprenticeship program but to build on the current programs, most potential opposition to the bill faded away. The construction trades had been concerned with the use of the term "apprenticeship" because they had adult apprenticeship programs of long standing, but the shift in policy rendered their concern no longer relevant. The American Vocational Association had been concerned that a new system would duplicate the current vocational programs, but they were supportive of the idea of building on the current structures. The business community liked the whole concept from the beginning, because they had long been concerned with the lack of job readiness among high school graduates.

As mentioned by Senator Simon, the only real dispute among the organizations came when the National Governors' Association and the Council of Chief State School Officers locked horns over whether the governor or the state school superintendent would control planning and the funds. The final compromise was to give priority in funding to those states that showed the greatest cooperation within state. This battle is another sign of the recent interest by the governors in federal education policy.

Senator Kassebaum represented a significant — though not majority — point of view in the last Congress when she expressed concern about creating new programs when there already were so many and when all these programs had to be funded from the same "frozen" pot of money. This argument goes back to the point I made at the beginning of this chapter in noting the problems resulting from Clinton's strategy to create new programs and to want funding for them after he and the Congress had agreed to a budget freeze in order to reduce the deficit. Senator Kassebaum received the support of 31 senators in voting against the School-to-Work Act. That number included Senator Robert Byrd, the chairman of the Appropriations Committee, which has to contend most directly with this tension over funding.

But, all things considered, the progress of the School-to-Work Act through the Congress was smooth. The broad support for this legislation shows that policy makers realize that the United States must find a better way to prepare its youth for employment. The assertion is repeatedly made that we are the only industrialized country in the world that does not have a school-to-work transition system, and so agreement was reached relatively easily that we must start work on creating one.

Process. In the second book in this series, *Community Service and Student Loans,* readers saw the starkest example of how process determines policy. The National and Community Service Trust Fund Act went through the regular legislative process, was changed through amendments, and survived a filibuster in the Senate to achieve final enactment. By way of contrast, the change-over in student loan programs from relying on banks and secondary markets to being directly supported by the federal government was a more closed process. In that case, the amendments went through "budget reconciliation," which meant that all amendments were foreclosed in the full House of Representatives and filibusters were not permitted in the Senate. The final conference agreement also was a straight up-or-down vote with no changes being permitted. Therefore, the process used for the direct loan change-over helped to determine the outcome, as it was much less open to outside pressure than was the process used to achieve the enactment of the community service bill.

With the Goals 2000 bill, the House passed the legislation with relatively few changes, except for the amendments the Democrats agreed to accept in order to modify their own amendments that had been adopted in committee.

There were so few amendments because the bill was brought to the full House at the end of the session. Urgency to finish work on many other bills created pressure to limit debate. However, the willingness of the Republican leadership to accept a procedure limiting amendments was crucial in restricting the process. The minority party was pleased that the Democratic liberals responded to Riley's urgings by modifying their own amendments. Therefore, although several amendments were permitted, no damaging changes were made to the bill by the minority party.

The situation in the Senate was different. Senator Kennedy had modified the Administration's original bill to limit standards and so had secured the support of many Republicans. But he had to bring the bill to the full Senate, where it was open to any amendments. The Senate has no rule of germaneness for amendments to bills, so any senator may offer any amendment he or she desires to any bill absent a unanimous consent agreement forbidding that procedure. Therefore, the Senate adopted amendments to the Goals 2000 bill forbidding guns in schools, requiring schools to have three different policies on permitting prayer, and restricting the giving of advice to students on using condoms.

Because of their more restricted procedure used to consider the bill, the House had none of these amendments. Therefore, the Senate-House conference committee was able to drop or change most of the non-germane Senate amendments. However, when it modified the amendment on school prayer that had been offered by Senator Helms, it imperiled the entire conference report. In the House, the Democratic leadership had to work very hard to secure acceptance of the report; and in the Senate, the Democratic leadership had to keep the Senate in session past midnight and into the Easter-Passover recess in order to break a filibuster mounted by Helms to oppose that deletion. If the House had not accepted the bill under a rule forbidding most amendments, the conference committee probably would not have been able to reject those amendments or change them, because they also could have been inserted into the House-passed version. This is an apt example of how process helps to determine outcome.

The School-to-Work Act, again, was simpler. In the House, the bill was taken up under a procedure barring any amendments. This was possible because of the broad bipartisan and organizational support for the bill. In the Senate, the bill immediately followed the lengthy consideration of the Goals legislation; it was easier to get a unanimous consent agreement limiting time for debate because so much time had been spent on the related Goals 2000 Act. Senator Kassebaum offered her amendments, but there was little other controversy on the bill. If the Senate had considered the School-to-Work bill at another time, there might have been lengthier debate and possibly additional amendments, including non-germane ones.

These comments have dealt with the procedural considerations involving the Goals 2000 and the School-to-Work Acts as they made their way through the legislative process. But an interesting question can be asked: What might have happened to the substance of these two new acts if they had been proposed as one bill instead of as two separate pieces of legislation?

Both bills as proposed by the President made some references to each other. Yet they are not intimately tied together. The Congress made some changes to the bills to try to bring them closer together, but they are still separate policies. The reason they are separate is that two different task forces worked on them in the Clinton Administration. The Goals group was composed solely of Department of Education staff, whereas the School-to-Work group was made up of staff from both the Departments of Education and Labor. When the bills were submitted to the Congress, they were referred to the same full committees but to different subcommittees. The Goals bill went to the education subcommittees in the House and the Senate, and the School-to-Work bill went to the job training subcommittees.

The separation in policy began in the executive branch of government and continued in the legislative branch, resulting in two different laws, both of which call for reforms in secondary schools. The states will face problems in trying to reconcile these two new policies because the two laws vest authority in somewhat different groups at the state level. Hopefully, enlightened state officials will see the overlap in policies and will reconcile any differences without unnecessary duplication of effort. The new laws do encourage the federal departments to try to foster a union of the state plans under these two laws.

I point out this separation of these two new laws because it resulted from the process by which the Administration and then the Congress chose to form them. With some wisdom and foresight, the states and the federal departments will minimize any conflicts between these two laws. This is another situation in which the process adopted for making policy makes a difference in the content of that policy.

Conclusion

Most discussions of current school reform begin with a reference to the *Nation at Risk* report of 1983, because that document galvanized afresh the drive to make American schools better. The irony of that report is that, although it was initiated by a U.S. Secretary of Education, Terrel Bell, and was released at the White House by a President, Ronald Reagan, it resulted in no federal action to help in that reform. Reagan, who was a firm believer that the federal government had no real role in education, had tried to eliminate the Department of Education and to repeal many federal programs, and so he was not inclined to mount any new national school reform effort.

Another Republican President, George Bush, began the movement away from Reagan's philosophy when he convened the summit conference on education with the nation's governors in 1989. Then he accelerated the shift in policy when he endorsed the idea of developing national content standards for education. But his legislative proposals were killed in the Congress because of conservative concerns about national control of education.

It took a Democratic President, Bill Clinton, to work with a Democratic Congress to secure enactment of national school reform legislation, but only after he had secured significant support from Republican congressmen. And the Congress has provided significant funding for both efforts — not as much as Clinton proposed — even though these funds had to be shifted from other federal activities to the Goals 2000 and School-to-Work Acts because of the five-year funding freeze adopted in 1993. Consequently, a decade after *A Nation at Risk* called for a national reform effort, the federal government finally has become a significant partner with the states and local school districts in upgrading education.

I would like to thank all the writers who gave freely of their talents and time to contribute to this book that, I hope, clearly explains how the national role in education has evolved to provide assistance to school reform. These writers all share with me the desire to explain how these new policies were developed so that those who are charged with carrying them out will understand the reasoning, the politics, and the processes that shaped them.